Design Innovation for Health and Medicine

Erez Nusem
Karla Straker • Cara Wrigley

Design Innovation for Health and Medicine

Erez Nusem
School of Architecture, Design
and Planning
University of Sydney
Sydney, NSW, Australia

Karla Straker
School of Architecture, Design
and Planning
University of Sydney
Sydney, NSW, Australia

Cara Wrigley
School of Architecture, Design
and Planning
University of Sydney
Sydney, NSW, Australia

ISBN 978-981-15-4361-6   ISBN 978-981-15-4362-3   (eBook)
https://doi.org/10.1007/978-981-15-4362-3

This Palgrave Macmillan imprint is published by the registered company Springer Nature Singapore Pte Ltd.
The registered company address is: 152 Beach Road, #21-01/04 Gateway East, Singapore 189721, Singapore

Foreword

Medical devices are diverse, ranging from stethoscopes to artificial joints to hearts that are totally artificial. The more complex they are, the higher the risk of failure—which is often fatal for patients. The development of such devices is very complex in order to assess and mitigate risk, not least due to the required regulatory approval process, which may define up to 50 per cent of the development process.

As a biomedical engineer I was trained to find safe and effective technical solutions for clinical problems. In my early career as a researcher, I thought a problem was solved by a new or at least superior technology alone. I thought if a new heart valve produced a lower pressure gradient, it would be considered a success and be widely adopted. However, throughout my career as a researcher, inventor, developer and entrepreneur, I learned that it required far more than this problem-solution mindset. In order to successfully translate research into the clinical arena I had to learn that making something work once in a lab is relatively easy, and most of the time the engineering challenges are the easiest to solve. I learned about the Pareto principle[1] where 80 per cent of the result will come from just 20 per cent of the action. Meaning that the effort in the

---

[1] C. H. Powers, *Vilfredo Pareto* (Newbury Park, California: Sage Publications, 1987).

first proof of concept, with the first successful lab test to create a prototype, was only 20 per cent of the effort, getting us 80 per cent of the way to the final product. The remaining 80 per cent of the time, effort and costs would be required to achieve the final 20 per cent, getting to a fully functional product. And that may even be greatly understating things.

Along the journey to translation there are many pitfalls, and success depends on many factors. Reducing the risks of both the device itself and the development requires 'front loading': conscientiously planning all steps and processes. And it requires close collaboration of experts from many different disciplines: from clinicians to define the clinical requirements; engineers to design, test and manufacture the device; material scientists to select and even develop suitable materials; to regulatory affairs specialists for the approval process, and reimbursement specialists for developing a reimbursement strategy.

The best and newest valve with the lowest pressure gradient may fail if its material degrades in the human body or it cannot be kept sterile during storage. The best blood pump with the lowest blood damage may even kill patients if the controller produces misleading alarms and causes a nurse, a caregiver or the patient to take a wrong action. Unfortunately, these are not hypothetical scenarios.

The latter example underlines the often undervalued, but increasingly important, role of interaction, usability, ergonomics, experience and even appearance of medical devices. In short: the role of design. As the example shows, while usability can even be life-saving, it must also cater to diverse users. At the time of implantation, it is the surgeon; during hospitalisation it is the skilled nurse; after hospital discharge it may be the general practitioner, a layperson caregiver or even the patient themselves. Ergonomics is important, as quick and safe decisions may have to be made in stressful situations, e.g. surgery, intensive care or an emergency. Designers are trained to consider these factors and can offer immense value in the early stages of product development.

With the progressing digitalisation in health, the role of design will even gain further importance. While years ago an electrocardiogram (ECG) was recorded by special devices in hospitals or doctors offices by trained staff, it may nowadays be automatically recorded, at any time by anyone with a smartwatch, and stored in an electronic patient record. Medical products are now quickly merging with lifestyle products to become more and more personal. The dawn of a new era of medical devices is upon us and, as brilliant as engineers are at making things efficient, designers are needed more than ever to make sure they are effective.

Professor of Cardiovascular Engineering   Ulrich Steinseifer
Head, Department of Cardiovascular
Engineering CVE
Institute of Applied Medical Engineering AME
RWTH Aachen University, Aachen, Germany

Preface

As the challenges of healthcare become increasingly complex, new approaches are needed to address them. *Design Innovation in Health and Medicine* presents the case for a design approach to addressing such challenges, and to developing medical innovations. This book, unlike other books on this topic, is not a textbook. Rather, it is a book of case studies that explains and outlines different types of medical design innovation. It provides a framework for determining the best solution for any given problem or opportunity rather than a 'one size fits all' approach to medical solutions. The case studies in this book were selected from around the globe to highlight the applications of design in health and medicine. These cases, along with primary case studies directed by the authors in industry, outline the multidisciplinary approach to design, commercialisation and market research behind some of the world's most successful medical products, services and systems. The objective in writing this book was to share and disseminate knowledge as well as the authors' experiences as designers working alongside other professionals in the field of health and medicine. The hope is that others may accept design as a complementary method in their practice to create outcomes that improve patients' quality of life.

The purpose of this book is to illustrate the value of design in health and medicine by delving into the innovation process behind the case studies featured in the book. Emergent themes and contributions help medical engineers, clinicians and researchers learn how to apply design during the early stages of conceptualisation in order to achieve better, patient-centric outcomes.

Sydney, NSW, Australia

Erez Nusem
Karla Straker
Cara Wrigley

Setting the Scene

Medicine can treat the disease;
great medicine treats the patient who has the disease.
(based on a quote from Sir William Osler 1849–1919)

In a recent collaboration our team explored the experience of patients with ventricular assist devices—surgically implanted devices used to sustain the heart's circulatory function in patients with heart failure. As part of this project a researcher collected a decommissioned ventricular assist device and external battery pack from an interstate hospital. The researcher was waiting to go through airport security to fly back to Sydney when the device's alarm went off, distressing not only the researcher but also three airport security guards. The alarm, similar in volume to a car alarm, had begun ringing to indicate the device needed to be recharged. With the alarm blaring the researcher had to explain that the noise was caused by a medical device, not the airport security system detecting a bomb. While the situation was stressful, at least the researcher knew that there was no concern of an imminent medical emergency; there was little to fear beyond the initial awkwardness of the situation. But imagine if this had happened to a patient, who would likely be at significant risk of death if the implanted device were to be disconnected from the external battery in a similar chaotic situation.

When this experience was shared with the engineer who had provided the device, their response was that the device shouldn't be in airports or high-security areas. This implied that the fault lay with the user. But an argument could be made that a well-considered design would have eliminated the issue altogether. As this situation shows, despite being a feat of engineering with a brilliant technical design, the device had significant issues with the user experience. A new design for the device's wearable component was sketched up and sent back to the engineer that day. The fix was simple: just adding a medical symbol to the bag to indicate the type of device it contained.

As our societies continue to emphasise the need for 'patient-centric' healthcare systems and to embrace technology as innovation, we must stop and consider whether we are improving outcomes and experiences for patients and clinicians, or if healthcare is becoming transactional and impersonal. Our focus as medical practitioners, designers, engineers and other stakeholders must shift from not only prolonging life, but to also designing ways of improving it.

The concept of 'design' doesn't immediately come to mind when thinking in the parameters of health and medicine. Yet design is everywhere. It's in the products and services that we use, in the ways that we interact with systems, the ways in which we acquire information or receive data, and in the environments and experiences that make up our days. Almost every facet of our lives has been designed, and not necessarily by a designer. In health and medicine especially, design's role is not solely about making things look attractive. Through design we aim to improve outcomes for patients and clinicians, and challenge not just *why* things are, but also *how* things could be.

Design methodologies are being used to explore a wider range of products, services, processes and systems, in a wider range of industries, than ever before. Design, as a method for addressing stakeholder needs and problem solving, has also been established as a source of innovation.[1] Organisations depend on successful innovation to thrive, meet the needs

---

[1] Cara Wrigley, "Design Innovation Catalysts : Education and Impact," *She Ji: The Journal of Design, Economics, and Innovation* 2, no. 2 (2016): 148–65; Hasso Plattner, Christoph Meinel, and Larry Leifer, eds., *Design Thinking Research: Building Innovators, Understanding Innovation*, 1st ed. (Springer, 2014).

of their stakeholders and remain competitive—yet innovation is often viewed as a luxury or burden, even in fields such as healthcare, when it should be seen as a core activity.[2] Applications of design in healthcare, while established, are mostly conventional (e.g. medical engineering or architecture). Consequently, many unrealised opportunities remain. Nevertheless, healthcare organisations and research groups on a global scale are beginning to recognise the value of design. They are incorporating design processes into their practices with the aim of improving outcomes for patients and medical professionals alike.

This book has been driven by a need that we have seen in practice today. As design researchers we have been fortunate to work with a team of world-leading medical practitioners to explore a multitude of healthcare challenges and opportunities, and to develop approaches that can assist in addressing these. While many books provide explanations of the processes of designing medical products or even isolated systems, few discuss design holistically. This book has been written for anyone with an interest in medical design, with the aim of demonstrating design's role in creating value in healthcare, and sharing how design can contribute to the practice of healthcare.

---

[2] Lawton Robert Burns, *The Business of Healthcare Innovation*, 2nd ed. (Cambridge University Press, 2012).

Acknowledgements

Writing a book for a multi-disciplinary audience with varying degrees of education can be a difficult task. Indeed, such a task would not have been possible without the support of a number of people, whose contributions are acknowledged here.

We wish to thank Brittany Daws for her assistance in conducting background research for the manuscript. Kimmi Keum Hee Ko, Ling Yi Feng, Natalia Gulbransen-Diaz, Rachel Montgomery, Mackenzie Etherington and Jessica Lea Dunn for their contributions to the ventricular assist device project. Lindsay Page and Miranda Phillips for their work in the gestational diabetes project. Tamarra Mills, for her belief in and support of design—even when the engineers called for order. Dr Shaun Gregory (and his thick engineering skin) for his continued support and for detailed feedback throughout our collaborative endeavours. Dr Sean Peel for reviewing the manuscript.

Acknowledgement to The University of Sydney School of Architecture, Design & Planning. We also wish to thank Westmead Hospital for their belief in design and for the ongoing collaboration between our faculties.

The authors would like to recognise the financial assistance provided by The Prince Charles Hospital Foundation (TM2017-04) and the National Health and Medical Research Council Centre for Research Excellence (APP1079421/GNT1079421) for research conducted in the 'machines that keep the heart pumping' case study in Chap. 9.

We are grateful to our loved ones, family and friends for their unwavering support and encouragement.

Finally, to patients around the globe—we hope that this research can make a difference in improving clinical outcomes and quality of life.

Erez, Karla and Cara

Contents

About the Authors

The authors reside at the University of Sydney's School of Architecture, Design and Planning in the Design Innovation Research Group. Collectively, their research spans design innovation across a number of disciplines and has been detailed in a range of cross-disciplinary publications.

Through collaborations with start-up organisations, small-to-medium size enterprises and the multi-national corporate sector the authors investigate design methods, the implementation of design and the integration of design in practice. The authors have also collaboratively designed, implemented and established a new Design Major and Master of Design at the University of Sydney, through which they share insights from their practice.

Dr Erez Nusem emphasises the value of design in realising social and economic outcomes, with a focus on organisational change and design integration through longitudinal embedded projects. Through his engagements he has worked with hospitals, aged care providers and government entities. Most recently, he practiced at Westmead Hospital where design was disseminated as a strategic priority in order to better address patients' and clinicians' needs.

Dr Karla Straker researches in a cross-disciplinary setting exploring the design of digital channel engagements, investigated through theoretical approaches from the fields of design, psychology and marketing. Her research aims to understand how strong relationships with customers can be built and sustained through a deeper understanding of customer emotions. She is also the co-author of the books *Affected: emotionally engaging customers in the digital age* published by Wiley, and *Design. Think. Make. Break. Repeat* published by BIS.

Professor Cara Wrigley is the Director of the Design Innovation Research Group, leading a team of researchers on projects spanning healthcare, science, business and defence. She investigates the application and adoption of design innovation methods by various industry sectors in order to research the value that design holds in business—specifically through the creation of strategies to design business models which lead to emotive customer engagement. She is a prolific publisher and leader in this field.

List of Figures

List of Tables

1

Medical Design

The Design and Development of Products for Health or Medical Purposes

Design is often interrelated with engineering in the disciplines of health and medicine, and is typically represented by medical products and devices created by medical engineers or 'mechanical designers'—a mix of mechanical engineering and industrial design. Such medical products and devices have often favoured technological advancement over 'design' and patients' needs and requirements. Despite a preoccupation with technical solutions, engineers sometimes refer to themselves as 'designers', resulting in a great deal of confusion about what design actually is, who practises it and how. It's important to note that engineers and designers approach design in fundamentally different ways.

Take for example the product AcceleGlove, created by Jose Hernandez-Rebollar of George Washington University to 'translate' sign language into text and speech (see Fig. 1.1 for an early iteration of the device). The basic concept for this wearable technology dates back to the early 1980s, when engineers from Bell Labs in the USA explored human–computer interaction through gestures, which later led to the invention of a glove that used the 26 manual gestures of the American Manual

© The Author(s) 2020
E. Nusem et al., *Design Innovation for Health and Medicine*,
https://doi.org/10.1007/978-981-15-4362-3_1

Fig. 1.1   AcceleGlove

Alphabet for data entry.[1] The engineers' intent was that the AcceleGlove be used to simplify interactions between those with a hearing disability and those without, claiming that the device could translate American sign language. However, the glove's design and technologies overlooked the intricacies of sign language. The glove was only able to translate individual letters, not the full range of signs commonly used. AcceleGlove was designed on a set of assumptions that didn't reflect the needs of deaf signers.

Engineers are taught to isolate a problem and focus on the detail. While this is a necessary and important method in some fields of work, it can overlook the intricacies critical to the success of products used in social or day-to-day contexts. In the instance of this technology, the engineers focused primarily on what the hands do, rather than on how deaf people receive and send information (i.e., how they communicate). They also failed to consider the broader social context in which the device would be used. Similar products such as SignAloud and the BrightSign Glove have been developed more recently, leveraging modern

---

[1] The AcceleGlove case study is based on an article written by Michael Erard. For more information, see Michael Erard, "Why Sign-Language Gloves Don't Help Deaf People," The Atlantic, 2017, https://www.theatlantic.com/https://www.theatlantic.com/.

Fig. 1.2 The engineering design process

technologies such as machine learning. However, these still fail to capture the nuances of individual signers.[2]

Design, as practised by engineers and demonstrated in the previous example, is traditionally driven by a problem presented by a clinician. The design process is guided by a Quality Management System[3] which frames clinicians as the 'users'. While the patient problem is known, patients are not explicitly consulted and their needs are largely assumed. In such a scenario, an engineer takes the problem and works towards a solution. The problem and solution are both concrete—i.e., tangible things that an engineer can grapple with. Such a process is illustrated in Fig. 1.2.

On the other hand, holistic design processes also grapple with the abstract: the insights and ideas that might inform a solution. This abstract realm is where a designer challenges their own assumptions in relation to the problem, gathers insights from stakeholders (such as patients) and tests their thinking and ideas objectively. It can be difficult to recognise the value of these activities, as the outcomes can often be intangible. However, these activities often lead to a more profound understanding of a problem (or even lead to a different, previously overlooked problem that needs to be addressed). These methods allow designers to question *why* a problem exists, rather than purely focusing on how it can be addressed, and result in far improved, and at times radically different, solutions. It can be challenging to demonstrate the value that design

[2] Keith Kirkpatrick, "Technology for the Deaf," *Communications of the ACM* 61, no. 12 (2018): 16–18.

[3] ISO 13485:2016 Medical devices—Quality management systems—Requirements for regulatory purposes. Available at https://www.iso.org/.

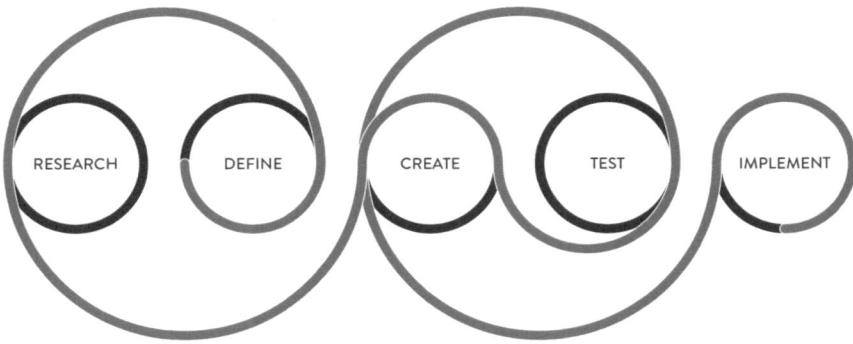

Fig. 1.3 The design process

offers in healthcare; it requires an open discourse and shared understanding of not only how these outcomes can be achieved, but also the very meaning of 'design'.

As a term 'design process' is somewhat of an oxymoron. Indeed, defining standard practice for something inherently creative is a challenge. However, there are a number of phases—research, define, create, test and implement—that generally take place in the design of new products, services or systems. As design is iterative and at times ambiguous, these phases do not always occur in the same order. For example, as shown in Fig. 1.3, sometimes design may begin with defining the problem, followed by research, the conception of solutions, testing, revision or redesign of the solution(s), and finish with implementation.

2

Describing Design

The word 'design' has many uses. As the discipline of design has evolved the role of design as a verb—i.e., the actions and thoughts involved in the process of designing—has become increasingly prominent. Building on Heskett's work,[1] we refer to design in three ways:

- as a noun, depicting the field or discipline of design
- as a noun, referring to a design output (a tangible or intangible artefact that has been designed)
- as a verb.

As a Noun

Design comes in many forms, and is comprised of numerous disciplines (e.g. architectural design, industrial design, graphic design, etc.). One prominent model that summarises the various outputs of design is Buchanan's four orders of design (see Fig. 2.1). There is ongoing debate

---

[1] John Heskett, "Past, Present, and Future in Design for Industry," *Design Issues* 17, no. 1 (2001): 18–26.

© The Author(s) 2020
E. Nusem et al., *Design Innovation for Health and Medicine*,
https://doi.org/10.1007/978-981-15-4362-3_2

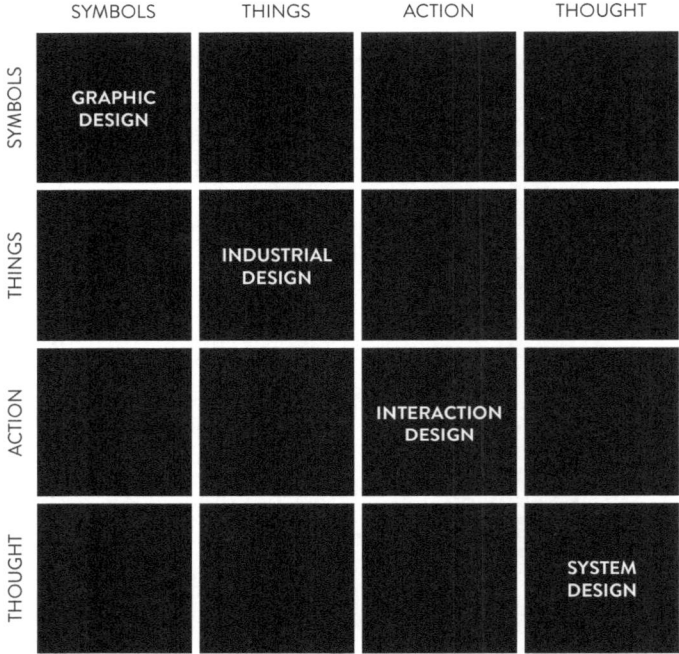

Fig. 2.1 The four orders of design (adapted from Buchanan 2001)

in design surrounding the role of tradition and innovation, and this model was introduced in part as a response to that debate. Buchanan, when introducing the four orders, described the output of design as artefacts that represent 'information, activities, service, and policies, as well as systems' emerging from the design process.[2]

These four orders describe the types of artefacts expected as outputs from the design process, as well as the disciplines of design from which such artefacts emerge. The first order is 'symbols', referring to the communication of information through text or imagery emerging from the discipline of graphic design. The second order focuses on the creation of 'things', i.e. the design of material objects, that emerge from the discipline of industrial design. The third order is concerned with the

---

[2] Richard Buchanan, "Design Research and the New Learning," *Design Issues* 17, no. 4 (2001): 7.

design of 'action' and interaction, the mediation of interaction between human beings through or with a 'product'. This form of design sits under the umbrella of 'interaction design': service design as well as user experience and interface design. The fourth order, as described by Buchanan, attends to '[t]he idea or thought that organizes a system or environment'.[3] In other words, the fourth order of design encompasses the environments and systems in which all other orders of design exist. Therefore the emphasis is on human systems, along with 'the integration of information, physical artefacts, and interactions in environments of living, working, playing, and learning'. We now discuss the role of these orders in health and medicine.

The First Order of Design

The first order is that of graphic design, and visual symbols that communicate information through the use of words and images. An example is the logo for Cochlear—an organisation specialising in surgically implanted neuroprosthetic devices that simulate sound for those with hearing loss.[4] Seen in Fig. 2.2, the logo is a symbolic representation of ear anatomy. Through the use of the first order of design, Cochlear is also able to articulate their vision as 'Hear Now. And Always'. Their slogan demonstrates their focus on the recipients of their products and their families, and makes their purpose explicit, cementing the association

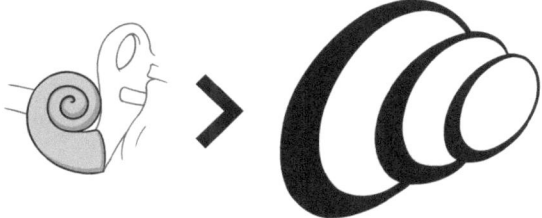

Fig. 2.2 Cochlear logo abstraction

---

[3] Buchanan, 12.

[4] Fan-Gang Zeng, Stephen Rebscher, William Harrison, Xiaoan Sun, and Haihong Feng. "Cochlear Implants: System Design, Integration, and Evaluation." *IEEE Reviews in Biomedical Engineering* 1 (2008): 115–42.

with their name and their product. Following this strategy has allowed Cochlear to maintain their position as market leaders for decades.

The Second Order of Design

The second order of design is that of industrial design and the design of 'things', i.e., physical and tangible objects. One example is the Hue Inhaler designed by Tim Zarki (see Fig. 2.3).[5] Here, design was used as an approach to re-imagine the asthma puffer—a device to assist patients suffering from asthma. The intent of the design was to eliminate the stigma associated with the puffer through an aesthetic transformation. The medical device became a product more akin to a fashion accessory, and the functional inclusion of a cord allowed the device to be attached to other objects. In this case, design was used to reconceptualise the emotional stigma related to asthma, influencing the form, materials, usability, branding, interaction and the aesthetics of the device.

Fig. 2.3   Traditional inhaler (left) and Hue inhaler (right)

---

[5] For additional information see 'Hue Inhaler' on Tim Zarki's portfolio at https://www.behance.net/.

The Third Order of Design

The third order of design is concerned with interactions, i.e., human experiences. An example described by Verganti[6] is the use of computed tomography scanners (CT scanners)—medical imaging systems that allow users to see inside an object, such as a patient, without the need for cutting.[7] Such scanners required relatively lengthy exposure, during which patients must remain still. The response to this challenge was to take measures to reduce exposure time, despite this resulting in a higher dose of radiation for patients. Instead the designers at Philips, a major manufacturer of these scanners, shifted the focus from technological innovation to the patient's emotional state during the scanning procedure. By focusing on the experience of the patient during their interaction with the technology, the designers were able to remove anxiety from the procedure and produce a more pleasant and relaxing experience for patients. In the case of child patients, in particular, this reduced scan times (and therefore patients' exposure to radiation) and the need for sedation.

The Fourth Order of Design

The fourth order of design is used to explore environments (and the systems therein). One simple example of fourth-order design is a hospital. A hospital provides a physical environment where the ill and wounded can be treated, and is supported by a number of systems—from those used within a hospital, such as triage (the assessment of wounds or illness to determine the order of treatment for patients), to the larger systems of which the hospital itself is a part (i.e., the group of entities that collectively deliver health and medical services to a populace).

Throughout this book the four orders of design are used to frame the design outputs being discussed, along with the discipline(s) from which the outputs emerged. These orders allow us to structure our discussion of

---

[6] Roberto Verganti, "Designing Breakthrough Products: How Companies Can Systematically Create Innovations That Customers Don't Even Know They Want," *Harvard Business Review* 89, no. 10 (2011): 114–20.

[7] This example is discussed in more detail in Chapter 4 (p. 34).

design for health and medicine, and contribute to our medical design innovation framework (as detailed in Part II of the book).

As a Verb

In recent times it has become understood that design can add value beyond the development of products and services.[8] Indeed, design is progressively being adopted as a method of problem solving and conceptualising solutions that address the needs of all stakeholders—even in areas that are not traditionally seen as the domain of design.[9] One such methodology is design innovation. Positioned at the intersection of design thinking, strategic innovation and business management, design innovation serves as a way to adapt and respond to emerging challenges in health and medicine. This is achieved by looking beyond the immediate concerns of a challenge or opportunity, thus ensuring that the right dimensions are addressed.[10] In health and medicine, design innovation takes place across four stages (see Fig. 2.4). These four stages are defined as:

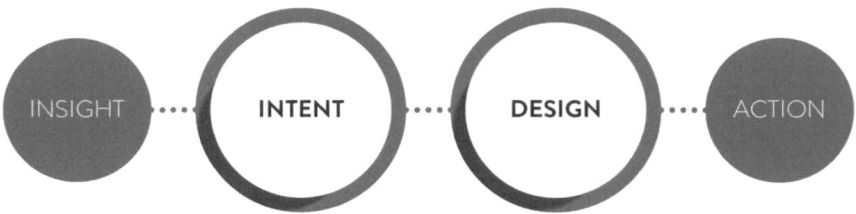

Fig. 2.4   Key components of design innovation in health and medicine

[8] Brigitte Borja Mozota, "The Four Powers of Design: A Value Model in Design Management," *Design Management Review* 17, no. 2 (2010): 44–53; Bettina Von Stamm, *Managing Innovation, Design and Creativity* (Chichester, New York: John Wiley & Sons, 2003).

[9] Tim Brown and Jocelyn Wyatt, "Design Thinking for Social Innovation," *Stanford Social Innovation Review* 8, no. 1 (2010): 31–36; Kees Dorst, *Frame Innovation: Create New Thinking by Design* (Cambridge, Massachusetts: MIT Press, 2015).

[10] James Carlopio, "Creating Strategy by Design," *Design Principles and Practices: An International Journal* 3, no. 5 (2009): 155–66; Matthew Holloway, "How Tangible Is Your Strategy? How Design Thinking Can Turn Your Strategy into Reality," *Journal of Business Strategy* 30, no. 2/3 (2009): 50–56.

- **Insight:** the information that informs or inspires a design, which can be the result of an audit using secondary or primary data
- **Intent:** the intended outcome of designing, which is informed by the insights captured
- **Design:** designing and 'scaffolding' the design output using the four orders of design
- **Action:** implementing and evaluating the design.

To provide a quick explanation of this process we will use our case study on Bravo, a service designed by an aged care provider to foster positive ageing behaviours and extend healthy life expectancy for the elderly.[11] The provider knew it needed to shift from its homogeneous business model and adapt to changing regulatory conditions, an ageing population and customers with increasing demands. It formed its **insight** through an investigation of its competitive landscape and research into its target demographic. These activities revealed a desire for aged care to shift from a disease focus (reactive) to a holistic wellbeing focus (proactive). The organisation then framed its **intent**, which was to redefine the ageing experience by empowering the elderly. The **design** process consisted of the organisation: testing its assumptions and findings from preliminary research; conceptualising ideas that would better align to future customer needs; and creating a prototype for evaluation with customers. Ultimately, the design sought to guide positive behavioural change through a business model offering advice, motivation and connection. **Action** was then taken with Bravo being launched as a start-up with a small customer base.

As illustrated by this example, design can serve as a method for conceptualising innovative ideas and navigating complex ecosystems—which is particularly relevant for healthcare innovation, as it requires the consideration of a host of determinants (e.g. ethical, economic and regulatory) for successful implementation. The Bravo case study is presented here as a simple example of the four stages of design innovation for health and medicine.

---

[11] As articulated by the organisation's Chief Customer Officer in "'Bravo' to RSL Care!", Aged Care Guide (2015), https://www.agedcareguide.com.au/.

In a field with high risk and human implications, organisations must adhere to copious standards and guidelines,[12] with approval for new designs taking a significant amount of time and money. Despite being necessary, these delays pose a challenge for new technologies and entrants to market; therefore, in Part II we introduce a framework to assist in navigating these complex challenges. Design innovation serves to balance these complexities, and consider the synergy of product, service and system outputs to mediate the needs of patients and practitioners.

Book Structure

As suggested in Fig. 2.4, this book has two primary foci—intent and design—and is thus segmented across two parts. Part I of the book focuses on intent, outlining a number of case studies that depict the outputs and outcomes of design in health and medicine. This portion of the book begins with an introduction and definition for each of the outcomes that have been identified, and provides case studies to demonstrate these outcomes. The case studies outline how design was used in a variety of medical contexts, and present the value and potential shortcomings of design in the medical sector. Part I also details design considerations derived from the case studies, to help inform readers' own design practices.

In Part I we describe and illustrate a model that captures the four outcomes of design in health and medicine:

- capacity
- knowledge
- enablement
- empowerment.

Part II focuses on 'design', introducing the medical design innovation framework in further detail and illustrating its application through a number of case studies conducted by the authors. In Part II we describe the design innovation process, with a focus on the:

---

[12] For examples of these standards and guidelines see the Food and Drug Administration (FDA) and Therapeutic Goods Administration (TGA).

- context of the design
- intended outcomes of design
- types of design that might be utilised.

Three primary case studies are used to demonstrate the medical design innovation process. These cases detail the activities undertaken by the authors and how the disciplines of design were used. Finally, we elaborate on the evolving role of design in health and medicine.

This book is not just about presenting case studies on medical designs that have been successfully taken to market; it is about explaining the story behind these designs, as this is just as important as the designs themselves. We have written this book as a resource for students, academics and practitioners to develop an understanding of the role design plays in health and medicine, and to provide inspiration for the future of design in this context. Our hope is that the frameworks outlined in this book will be used to structure future design work in health and medicine. Perhaps most importantly, this book seeks to create a dialogue that bridges two often disparate fields: design and healthcare.

Part I

Intent

3

Design Outcomes in Health and Medicine

The healthcare sector is complex, with ample challenges and opportunities. Given the value that design has demonstrated in many global sectors, there is much to gain by harnessing design to realise outcomes for patients and medical staff alike. In this chapter we argue that for design to be successful, it is important to first consider its intended outcomes. The research outlined in Part I is based on the study of multiple cases, which provides a basis for qualitative comparison. We chose to use case studies because of their applicability in analysing modern and unique phenomena.[1] A total of 30 cases were selected to explore the ways in which design is used in health and medicine, and to demonstrate how design is utilised in our society to drive innovation.

Through our research we have observed the outcomes of design to be segmented across two dimensions. The first dimension is concerned with the driver for innovation, i.e., whether a design is driven by a challenge or opportunity. Design driven by a challenge implies a reactive approach, where an issue has arisen that needs to be addressed. Conversely, design driven by an opportunity implies a proactive approach, one concerned

---

[1] Robert K. Yin, *Case Study Research: Design and Methods*, 4th ed. (Thousand Oaks, California: Sage Publications, 2009).

© The Author(s) 2020
E. Nusem et al., *Design Innovation for Health and Medicine*,
https://doi.org/10.1007/978-981-15-4362-3_3

with overcoming, or preventing, potential issues. The second dimension outlines for whom the design is intended: internal (e.g. practitioner of healthcare) or external (e.g. recipient of healthcare) stakeholders. The four identified outcomes for design in health and medicine are shown in Fig. 3.1, with these outcomes segmented across the aforementioned dimensions.

The outcomes depicted in Fig. 3.1—capacity, knowledge, enablement and empowerment—are design's contributions in health and medicine. It is through these four outcomes that we begin to explore the cases detailed in the following chapters.

Capacity

The first outcome is design for *capacity*, where design is used to reduce strain on a medical entity (such as a hospital). Such innovations result in more timely services and assist the medical sector to cope with increasing demands. For example, a design might result in more efficient processes,

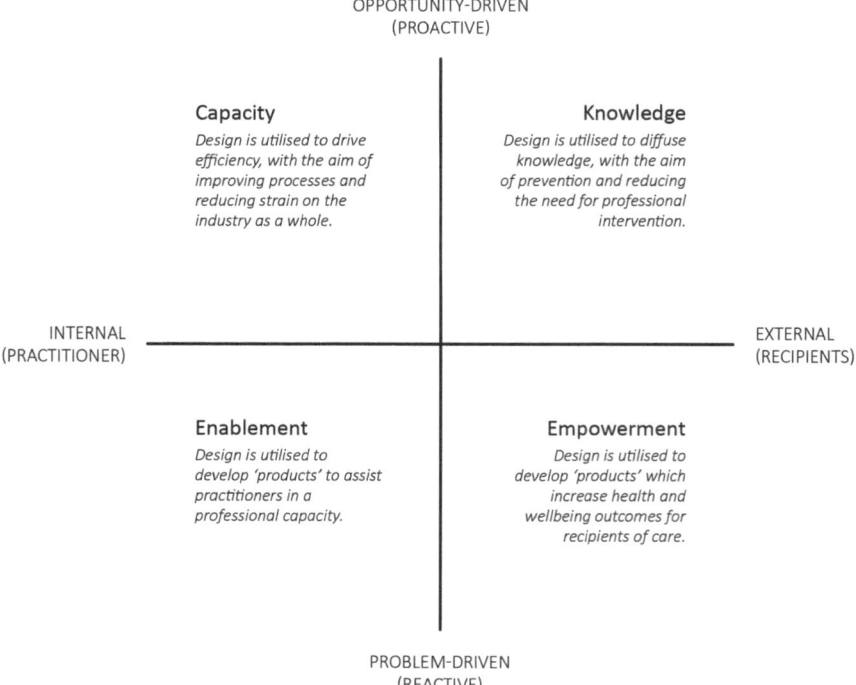

OPPORTUNITY-DRIVEN
(PROACTIVE)

Capacity

Design is utilised to drive efficiency, with the aim of improving processes and reducing strain on the industry as a whole.

Knowledge

Design is utilised to diffuse knowledge, with the aim of prevention and reducing the need for professional intervention.

INTERNAL
(PRACTITIONER)

EXTERNAL
(RECIPIENTS)

Enablement

Design is utilised to develop 'products' to assist practitioners in a professional capacity.

Empowerment

Design is utilised to develop 'products' which increase health and wellbeing outcomes for recipients of care.

PROBLEM-DRIVEN
(REACTIVE)

Fig. 3.1 Design outcomes for health and medicine

reducing handover time for nurses in between shifts,[2] or reducing the average time of a CT scan in order to reduce anxiety and distress in young patients.[3]

Knowledge

The second outcome is concerned with design for *knowledge*, where design is leveraged to inform the general public. The aim is to prevent or mitigate medical conditions, reducing the need for professional intervention, or raising awareness or funds (such as those used to conduct research and develop a cure). For example, the Ice Bucket Challenge, a social media campaign launched to raise awareness and funds to combat Amyotrophic Lateral Sclerosis.[4]

Enablement

The third outcome is concerned with the *enablement* of internal stakeholders through the design of 'products' to help practitioners deliver medical services. Examples include medical devices such as trocars,[5] which assist clinicians with surgical procedures, or tools and devices that assist with diagnostics, such as stethoscopes and ultrasound machines.[6]

Empowerment

The outcome of *empowerment* surrounds the wellbeing of healthcare recipients, for example the design of pen/self-injector drug delivery devices that instil confidence or reduce fear in users, or empowering

---

[2] T Brown, "Design Thinking," *Harvard Business Review* 86, no. 6 (June 2008): 84–92, 141.

[3] Donald A. Norman and Roberto Verganti, "Incremental and Radical Innovation: Design Research vs. Technology and Meaning Change," *Design Issues* 30, no. 1 (2014): 78–96.

[4] Hashem Koohy and Behrad Koohy, "A Lesson from the Ice Bucket Challenge: Using Social Networks to Publicize Science," *Frontiers in Genetics* 5, no. 430 (2014): 1–3.

[5] Frederic H. Moll, Alex T. Roth, Peter F. Costa, and William A. Holmes. Trocar. U.S. Patent 4,654,030. Washington, DC: U.S. Patent and Trademark Office, issued 1987.

[6] Paola Bertola and Jose Carlos Teixeira, "Design as a Knowledge Agent: How Design as a Knowledge Process Is Embedded into Organizations to Foster Innovation," *Design Studies* 24, no. 2 (2003): 181–94; Ariel Roguin, "Rene Theophile Hyacinthe Laënnec (1781–1826): The Man behind the Stethoscope," *Clinical Medicine and Research* 4, no. 3 (2006): 230–35.

individuals with disabilities or acute conditions to face adversity (e.g. cochlear hearing implants for the deaf, or Liftware eating utensils for individuals who have limited hand and arm mobility).

*   *   *

Design has led to a host of outputs spanning the aforementioned outcomes; examples are listed in Table 3.1. The design outputs have been

Table 3.1 Design cases and outcomes in health and medicine

Outcome	Typology	Case study
Design for capacity	Information systems	Concrn
		HealthMap
	System automation	Defibrillator and Zipline drones
		Driverless ambulances
	Efficiency innovations	Nurse handover
		CT scanner
Design for knowledge	Blueprints	Thrive: perceptions of hospitals
		Hospitable Hospice
	Awareness	Ice Bucket Challenge
		World's Greatest Shave
	Visual communication	Packaging pills
		Rescue Rashie
Design for enablement	Procedural instruments	Trocar
		3D Printing
		Pap smear speculum
	Diagnostics	Wong-Baker Pain Scale
		Stethoscope
		Ultrasound machine
Design for empowerment	Promoting ability	LiftWare
		Cochlear
		TickleFLEX
	Confidence instillers	EpiPen
		Tango Belt
	Experiential design	Tovertafel Original
		Kitten Scanner
		SnowWorld
		Incubator

classified according to a number of typologies we developed to best illustrate the types of design that contribute to each of the four outcomes discussed.

In the following chapters we present a comprehensive breakdown of each of the outcomes listed in Table 3.1, including the correlated typologies and case studies. For each of the case studies we explain:

- the context
- any notable changes over time
- the broader role and impact of design.

4

Design for Capacity

Capacity: Ability to Do

The core of the medical sector is the treatment and diagnosis of illness and injury. As an outcome, 'capacity' is defined by our ability to meet increasing demand, and to adapt and respond to our evolving environment. Increasing demands on the medical sector stem from a range of sources, including social changes, an ageing population, the development of new therapies (leading to new questions and requirements) and the integration of new technologies (leading to new fields of practice).

Social, scientific and technical advancements are also contributing to large-scale changes, constantly driving, extending and increasing the capacity of the medical sector. Meanwhile, hospitals and healthcare systems continue to prioritise reducing the overall cost of practice and increasing efficiency. These initiatives tie into the first outcome discussed in this book—design for capacity (see Fig. 4.1).

Design for capacity is often opportunity-driven and therefore tends to be proactive. Additionally, such innovations are designed with an internal frame of view, focusing on medical practitioners and professionals. Each of the four design outcomes listed in this book plays a role in ensuring

© The Author(s) 2020
E. Nusem et al., *Design Innovation for Health and Medicine*,
https://doi.org/10.1007/978-981-15-4362-3_4

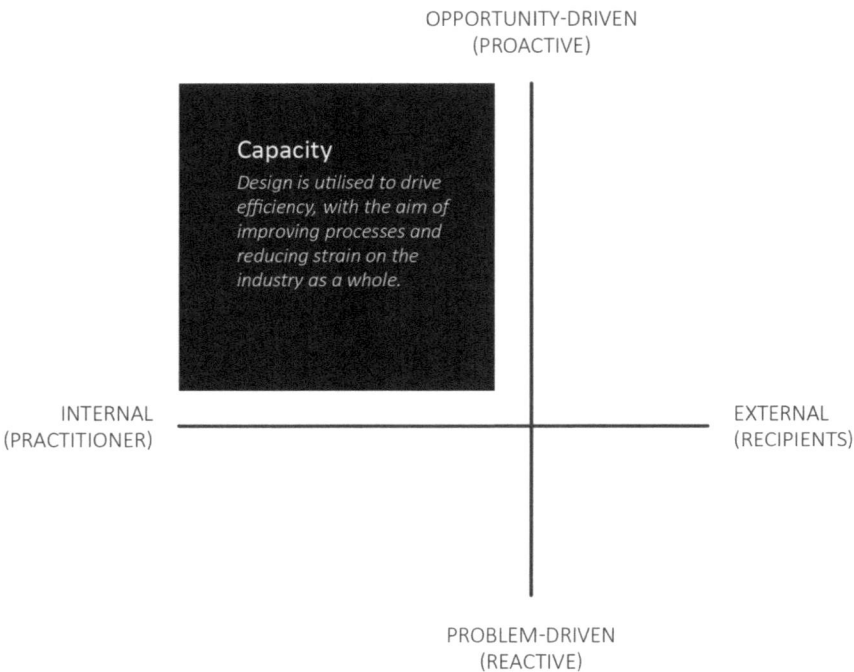

Fig. 4.1 Design for capacity

that the healthcare sector is able to cope with increasing demand as our society becomes ever more interconnected and developed. The outcome of capacity, in particular, plays a role in ensuring that our systems and processes are efficient and up to date. A number of design typologies realise this goal. Largely, these designs drive efficiency, and, more recently, automation. The case studies outlined in this chapter illustrate these points and showcase how each of the four orders of design is being used to drive capacity for healthcare.

We segment this chapter across three typologies, as detailed in Table 4.1. First, through *information systems*, which help the healthcare sector to cope with various challenges. Second, through service and *system automation* that provide more timely responses for medical emergencies. Finally, through *efficiency innovations* that improve the efficiency of

Table 4.1   Design for capacity overview

Design for capacity	Typology	Description	Case study
Design is utilised to reduce strain on a medical entity	Information Systems	Automated systems or interrelated components working together in the collection, processing, transition and dissemination of data	Concrn HealthMap
	System Automation	Process to be performed without human assistance, to reduce the need for human work in the process	Defibrillator and Zipline drones Driverless ambulances
	Efficiency Innovations	Reviewing processes and providing new and innovative approaches	Nurse handover CT scanner

medical interactions and processes. For each of these typologies we detail a number of case studies that demonstrate design for capacity.

Information Systems

Information systems are comprised of people, processes and technology. These systems are often automated, or feature interrelated components that work together in the collection, processing, transition and dissemination of data. One example is registration at a hospital. When you register, the information you provide is fed into an information system designed to support administrative reporting and processing. Information systems play a large role in ensuring that the medical sector is capable of responding to emerging challenges. These systems equip medical professionals with the information required to respond to a given situation. We use two examples to illustrate this typology: Concrn and HealthMap.

Concrn: Alternative Support for the Homeless

San Francisco's homelessness crisis is complex; there are a variety of other concerns stemming from the likes of hunger, mental illness and crime. In 2017 Concrn[1]—a mobile application described as 'compassionate crisis response for neighbours'—was developed to offer an alternative to calling 911 to get support for mental health crises, homelessness and substance abuse issues in the Tenderloin district in San Francisco.[2] This community-based crisis reporting application, developed by Jacob Savage and Neil Shah, identifies the homeless population of the Tenderloin district as a primary stakeholder.

Rather than seeking police aid, as was previously the norm, members of the public could use the mobile application to report homeless people in distress. A trained community member would then be alerted to help assist the distressed individual (see Fig. 4.2).

Fig. 4.2 Concrn storyboard

---

[1] The official website for Concrn can be found at https://www.concrn.org/.

[2] For more information on the homelessness crisis and the app Concrn, see Melia Robinson and Katie Canales, "San Francisco's Homelessness Crisis Is so Dire, There's Now a 911 Alternative to Get People on the Street Instant Help—Here's How It Works," Business Insider, 2018, https://www.businessinsider.com/.

While the application is relatively straightforward, the impact of Concrn is the way it transforms how individuals communicate with one another. Through the use of experience and systems design, Concrn has reframed how the public interacts with homeless individuals in distress—contributing positive outcomes in difficult situations. As a service integrated within a system, the community that Concrn has built is unique. Some Concrn responders have been homeless, so their past experiences and background allow them to empathise in their encounters with homeless people. Were Concrn to be a standalone mobile application, its impact would likely be diminished. Through the integration of the application within a system, Concrn provides the Tenderloin district in San Francisco the capacity to address the homelessness issue.

HealthMap: Disease Surveillance

HealthMap is an electronic information system created by a team of researchers,[3] software developers and epidemiologists at the Boston Children's Hospital in 2006, and has been established as a global leader in 'utilizing online informal sources for disease outbreaks',[22] The system provides users—including local health departments, governments and international travellers—real-time feedback and surveillance on emerging public health threats worldwide.

Since its inception, HealthMap has continued to improve through advances in technology and modern medicine, growing into one of the most important public health technologies and communication platforms for infectious diseases.[22] The system has remained relatively similar in function through the years, but has begun to push its data to additional audiences through mobile applications.

While originally a design from the fourth order of systems, HealthMap has relied on graphic design and interaction design through its development. In particular, in light of the increasing reliance on smartphones,

---

[3] For additional information see Clark C. Freifeld et al., "HealthMap: Global Infectious Disease Monitoring through Automated Classification and Visualization of Internet Media Reports," *Journal of the American Medical Informatics Association* 15, no. 2 (2008): 150–57. The HealthMap platform can be found at http://healthmap.org/.

HealthMap has seen an opportunity to create and evolve the original concept through a number of mobile applications. Amongst these applications are 'Flu Near You', 'Vaccine Finder', 'Outbreaks Near Me' and 'MedWatcher'—a drug safety app using the same technology as HealthMap. Nevertheless, at its core the service provided by HealthMap is the integration of two diverse systems: government-controlled information systems and media systems.

The role of design has evolved over the decades, especially with our increasing online presence rapidly transforming the way we live. HealthMap is an example of this, with the online platform changing the way people interact with infectious diseases—especially in developing countries.[4]

Capacity through Information Systems

The design of information systems is critical in today's environment, as these systems facilitate and translate information. The two examples discussed in this typology provide actionable information to relevant stakeholders (both patients and practitioners), allowing them to make informed decisions, respond to emerging challenges (e.g. a distressed homeless individual) or prepare for future challenges (e.g. an outbreak of a contagious virus). The two case studies predominantly rely on the fourth order of design and are therefore classified as systems. However, a critical component of each of these systems is how the information is conveyed and expressed. Both systems offer a platform for embedding and withdrawing information, and are informed by user preferences as to how information is communicated.

The design of symbols and interactions are both quite important in the design of information systems for the healthcare sector. Without consideration of these two orders the systems would be incapable of translating the information they hold to relevant stakeholders. The design of such

---

[4] See Ben Heubl, "HealthMap—Online Technology to Transform Public Health," Innovatemedtec, 2015, https://innovatemedtec.com/.

systems is critical in ensuring that our society is able to cope with demand going into the future. These two case studies illustrate the need for design to consider all stakeholder groups, along with emerging channels for engaging users.

System Automation

The assembly line at Ford Motor Company in 1913 is often cited as the first form of automation. In this book, we refer to automation as the use of technology to perform human processes, with the aim of reducing workload for humans. Many of our routine activities have been automated, but the healthcare industry has been slower to automate due to concern about safety risks. Automation is unlikely to replace doctors and nurses, yet it could be incorporated into processes to improve productivity. For example, automation has been successfully integrated into pharmacies through the use of machines to count medication, freeing up pharmacists to focus on clinical work.

Many of today's systems in healthcare require some degree of human input. While for some of these systems the input is at a high level, such as maintenance and overview, other systems cannot function without labourers. Emergency systems for example, are contingent on human input. In such systems, responses that are not timely present significant risk. While measures exist for assessing the urgency of a given situation, individuals must be available to make the assessment. Automation of these systems could not only lead to more timely responses, but could also result in lower fatality rates and higher emergency response rates. We illustrate this through two cases under development: defibrillator drones and driverless ambulances.

Drones: Rapid Response Aids

Emergency services can be slow and delayed due to a number of factors (e.g. staffing, traffic, difficulty of access, etc.). Defibrillator drones are but one example of how rapid technology advancements can deliver shorter response times and assist people who suffer from cardiac arrest. This example illustrates a network of drones designed by Alec Momont to improve the capacity of existing emergency infrastructure. Each drone is equipped with a defibrillator capable of saving lives (see Fig. 4.3) and can fly at almost 100 kilometres per hour, increasing chances of survival from 8 per cent to 80 per cent.[5] The drones also fold into a toolbox of emergency supplies, and can be deployed at any time to allow a bystander to use the defibrillator, thus increasing the patient's chances of survival.[6] Future implementations could serve other use cases such as drowning, diabetes, respiratory issues and traumas.[7]

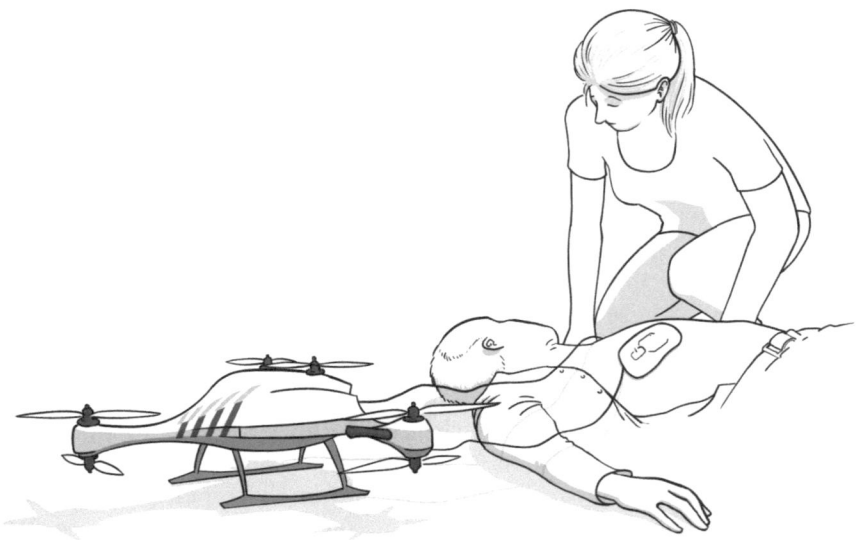

Fig. 4.3 Defibrillator drone

[5] For more information on defibrillator drones, see Larry Hueston, "Grad Student Invents Flying Ambulance Drone To Deliver Emergency Shocks," Forbes, 2014, https://www.forbes.com/.

[6] Andreas Claesson, Anders Bäckman, Mattias Ringh, Leif Svensson, Per Nordberg, Therese Djärv, and Jacob Hollenberg, "Time to Delivery of an Automated External Defibrillator Using a Drone for Simulated Out-of-Hospital Cardiac Arrests vs Emergency Medical Services," *Journal of the American Medical Association* 317, no. 22 (2017): 2332–34.

[7] Alec Momont, "Drones for Good" (Delft University of Technology, 2014).

Defibrillator drones use a number of design disciplines, including product design, experience design and systems design, to integrate patient and healthcare systems.[8] These disciplines have contributed to intuitive designs that address the current challenges that emergency response personnel face on a daily basis (such as timely access to patients). However, flightpath restrictions currently prevent drones from taking the optimal route and have been a major issue for implementation.[9] This issue could have been alleviated were the Civil Aviation Safety Authority (the body that governs flightpaths) identified as a key stakeholder and engaged and consulted earlier in the product development process.

Another drone currently providing medical aid is Zipline, a drone delivery system at national scale.[10] The drone (see Fig. 4.4) is dispatched via text message by health practitioners in remote areas, and it delivers medical supplies from a central distribution centre. Supplies are delivered in under 30 minutes after a confirmation text is sent, with packages being

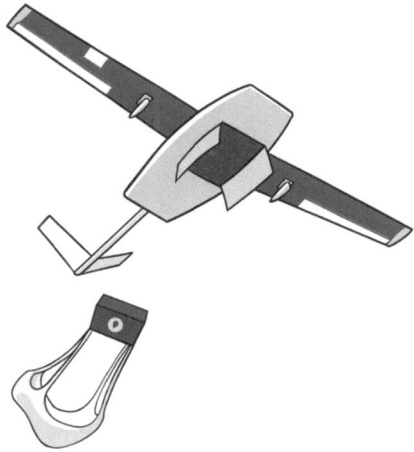

Fig. 4.4 Zipline drone

[8] Sam Wong, "Defibrillator Drones Could Save Lives before Ambulance Arrives," *New Scientist*, 2017, https://www.newscientist.com/.

[9] Anna Konert, Jacek Smereka, and Lukasz Szarpak, "The Use of Drones in Emergency Medicine: Practical and Legal Aspects," *Emergency Medicine International* 2019 (2019).

[10] More information on Zipline can be found at http://www.flyzipline.com/.

gently parachuted into a 'parking area' to be collected by practitioners. Zipline has refined their process through testing in different weather conditions and demand cycles, and now has the capacity to make 500 deliveries per day regardless of weather conditions. Zipline has the vision to build a delivery system for the planet and has recently developed an autonomous aircraft with improved speed and delivery capacity. They are currently working with key stakeholders (the US government and the FAA's National Airspace System) to overcome existing issues.

Driverless Ambulances: Redirection of Aid

Like defibrillator drones, driverless ambulances aim to improve emergency response time by allowing paramedics to categorise patients into states of need. Driverless ambulances can lessen the burden on emergency services by attending to low-risk situations, picking up patients and taking them to hospital. This increases the capacity of paramedics to treat high-risk patients.[11]

Driverless vehicles are becoming increasingly prevalent, with a multitude of systems being developed to support their integration into society. However, little is known about people's acceptance of riding in driverless vehicles.[12] Through design, we can begin to better understand stakeholders' perceptions of driverless vehicles and design outputs that are appropriate for distressed patients. Beyond the visualisation of this 'futuristic' mode of transport, which has long been a concern of industrial designers (along with the design of user-friendly and simplified interiors), there is a need to develop systems and wireless infrastructure to support driverless ambulances. Such systems would require constant updates and would need to be largely automated if they are to reduce strain on emergency services.

---

[11] Details on driverless ambulances are available via Keegan C Shepard, "In the Future Your Ambulance Could Be Driverless," The Conversation, 2017, https://theconversation.com/.

[12] For more information on trust and driverless ambulances, see Eddington, J. (2016) Julia Eddington, "Forget Cars—Would You Ever Trust a Driverless Ambulance?," The Zebra, 2016, https://www.thezebra.com/.

Capacity through System Automation

The two systems explored in this section outline efforts to automate critical systems in healthcare. Despite these being under development, the potential contributions of these systems are clear. These two cases provide examples of how design can be used to expand the role of existing products and services. Traditionally, both defibrillators (product), and ambulances (service) cannot function without medical practitioners. Nevertheless, their automation could result in a medical sector that is capable of making more timely responses to medical emergencies.

Efficiency Innovations

The healthcare sector relies on processes to ensure the streamlined delivery of medical services to patients. Given the high rates of regulation and conformity in healthcare, the review or innovation of services is often slow-moving and neglected. Processes can become sluggish, outdated or ill-considered. Design offers a means for reviewing these processes and providing new and innovative approaches. We explore efficiency innovations through two cases: the nurse handover procedure and the ambient experience for CT scanners.

Nurse Handover: New Procedures for Increasing Accuracy

In nursing, a handover is defined as the transfer of responsibility and accountability of patient care from one nurse or team of nurses to another.[13] During this procedure, nurses who are ending their shift are required to provide an update for nurses who are beginning their shift, with the aim of providing a seamless transition for patients and their families. The procedure has existed for as long as hospitals have, yet the execution of the procedure has changed to suit individual practitioners and institutions. Advances in technology and the evolution of procedures have

---

[13] British Medical Association, "Safe Handover: Safe Patients," *Guidance on Clinical Handover for Clinicians and Managers* (London: BMA, 2004).

resulted in significant changes to the procedure since the early twentieth century.

Brown[14] has described the issues Kaiser Permanente Healthcare hospitals had with nurse handover procedures. Nurses would often spend around 45 minutes of overtime debriefing the oncoming shift about the status of each patient. This exchange of information lacked structure, with each hospital featuring its own makeshift process for sharing and recording data—ranging from scribbles on the back of scrap paper to verbal recollections. This led to inconsistent communication, with vital patient information and treatment often being forgotten. Following a collaborative design workshop with multiple stakeholders, the hospitals came up with a new solution in the form of a portable software device. The device allowed nurses to pull up patient notes quickly and enabled nurses to change the location of the debrief to where the patients were (rather than the nurses' front station). Clear steps for easily interpreted communication have led to a high quality of knowledge transfer and increased the capacity of the incoming shift by halving the time required for handover.

CT Scanners: An Ambient Experience

Since the introduction of the CT scanner in the early 1970s radiologists have been demanding ever more powerful machines, with the aim of improving the quality of images and reducing the time and cost of examinations.[15] As radiographers have been perceived as the primary stakeholder, innovation has focused on devices that are more technologically sophisticated and efficient for imaging the body's internal structures. However, when the Philips design team got involved, they discovered an array of issues with the interaction between the machine and paediatric patients. Scanners required a relatively lengthy exposure, during which patients had to remain still. Anxious patients (especially children) often had to be sedated, increasing the duration of the procedure further.

---

[14]Tim Brown, "Design Thinking," *Harvard Business Review* 86, no. 6 (2008): 84–92.

[15]Roberto Verganti, "Designing Breakthrough Products: How Companies Can Systematically Create Innovations That Customers Don't Even Know They Want," *Harvard Business Review* 89, no. 10 (2011): 114–20.

Instead of focusing on the technology, which by this stage could produce high-resolution 3D views and inform detailed diagnoses,[16] designers shifted the focus to the patient's emotional state before and during the scanning procedure.[17]

Verganti[18] described how this resulted in the design of the 'ambient experience'—the integration of several technologies (such as LED displays, video animation, sensors and sound-control systems) to create a more relaxing atmosphere for patients. This was accomplished by designing a number of themes (e.g. 'aquatic' and 'nature') that would allow children to be immersed in the experience. Once a selection had been made, the child would be given a puppet with an RFID sensor that would automatically trigger theme-related animation, lighting and audio in the examination room. Nurses could then tailor a story around the projection to make the child feel immersed in the fictional environment, and teach them to stay still through the immersive experience. This simple change reduced the CT scan duration by 15–20 per cent, the number of children needing sedation by 30–40 per cent, and their radiation dose by 25–50 per cent.

Capacity through Efficiency Innovations

The role of design has changed alongside the evolution of the field, highlighting a shift in focus from technological advancements and ergonomic data to a focus on patients and their experiences. Notably, this also captures a shift in focus on the stakeholders for which we design, and the need to better consider for whom one is designing. As outlined in the nurse handover and ambient experience for CT scanners, design can be used to create more ideal experiences for patients and more efficient

---

[16] For more information on the history of CT imaging, see Philips, "Development of CT Imaging," 2006, https://www.philips.com/.

[17] Norman and Verganti, "Incremental and Radical Innovation: Design Research vs. Technology and Meaning Change."

[18] Verganti, "Designing Breakthrough Products: How Companies Can Systematically Create Innovations That Customers Don't Even Know They Want."

processes by better considering secondary stakeholders and reframing the focus of innovation.

Summarising Design for Capacity

In designing for capacity we aim to combat growing strains on the healthcare system. We outlined three typologies in design for capacity: *information systems*, *system automation* and *efficiency innovations*. Through these typologies we explored how the four orders of design are being used to improve capacity by:

- highlighting the need to better design our systems
- exploring the automation of practitioners for more timely services
- articulating the need to consider all stakeholders when improving our processes.

The impact and implications of design for capacity are numerous, including:

- the reduction of workload and labour
- improved quality and consistency in services
- reduced errors in healthcare
- improved capacity to deliver timely and informed healthcare services.

Designing for capacity should be seen as a way to separate a system into parts, and then examine the interactions between the parts. Understanding that individual elements exist within the whole system helps to identify interrelationships between elements. By dissecting a system in this way, it is possible to achieve vastly different solutions to problems that may not have been identified had the parts not been considered in isolation. Table 4.2 describes the four orders of design in this typology, providing examples of considerations and constraints to be noted when designing solutions for capacity.

Table 4.2 Design for capacity considerations and constraints

Order	Description	Considerations	Constraints
(1) Communication Design	Communication design for capacity is used as a means of explaining or indicating the purpose of the parts of a process or system, and to make sure that data is interpretable. It can also be used to communicate changes to processes or systems, illustrate the value added by changes, and develop a shared language across a family of designs (i.e., a number of integrated designs that support one another) through symbols.	• Displaying an appropriate amount of information • Users have varying degrees of comprehension and education • Use of symbols to communicate function and 'de-clutter' a busy interface • The multitude of ways in which data can be synthesised, some of which are more appropriate for users than others	• Design should align with current branding or rebranding • Pre-existing styles can impact acceptance and uptake of a design

(continued)

Table 4.2 (continued)

Order	Description	Considerations	Constraints
(2) Industrial Design	New products aren't just about leveraging new technologies, but also about ensuring that designs are accessible to a range of stakeholders. As we prioritise automation and autonomy, we have less manual oversight over who might need to use our products (e.g. the defibrillator drone). Industrial designs for capacity therefore need to be inclusive of the needs and requirements of a range of potential user groups.	• Appropriateness of product (i.e. usability, safety, ergonomics, etc.) for unknown stakeholders and users • Automation might require less human input, but not be cost effective • Testing with stakeholders is integral given the context of use (no guarantee of experienced user) • Reduced capacity to monitor condition of automated products (as a result of wear and tear, improper use or vandalism) due to potentially lessened input from professionals	• Reliance, reliability and safety of technology • Product design standards and regulations • Rate of technology updates, adoption and advancements • Cost influenced by low production rates and requirement of updates and improvements • User error

(3) Interaction Design	Technological advancements are often viewed as the most effective way to improve our capacity. However, simple interactions (which are often more readily implementable) can also have significant outcomes. Interactions for capacity are a fundamental aspect of ensuring that our systems are accessible and appropriate for users, and serve as the touchpoint for medical systems and services.	• Reliability, scalability and updatability are integral components of designing for automation • Interactions can help dictate and control the flow between different design components • The ease of interaction with automated designs is integral to their success. Understanding user needs and testing are therefore pivotal components	• Must balance user/ stakeholder safety and usability • Different ways of interpreting across people and cultures • Replicating human input without compromising function • Use of procedural and diagnostic instruments outside a medical context
(4) System Design	System design for capacity facilitates the connection between key components in systems and their external environment (i.e. regulatory bodies, context of use, etc.). Regulations or policies may inhibit implementation of proposed design solutions. For example, drones and autonomous vehicles must comply with flight paths and road rules respectively.	• System automations are not exclusively digital and can cater to a range of communities • Understanding existing deficits can highlight system design opportunities for capacity • Systems are complex, so it is best to eliminate or reduce processes that do not add value for stakeholders	• Existing laws and regulations influence system options • New systems should understand and integrate with existing systems without requiring human input

5

Design for Knowledge

Knowledge: Facts, Information and Skills

Design for knowledge (see Fig. 5.1) pertains to the use of design in establishing an informed society, with the aim of preventing medical conditions, reducing the need for professional intervention, and raising awareness or funds (such as those used to conduct research or develop cures for diseases). Educating society can have a tremendous impact on our healthcare systems, allowing individuals to take their health into their own hands. However, such education—defined as an intentional activity designed to transfer or construct knowledge about health to or for a person, social group or a community[1]—relies on a clear understanding of the dynamics of knowledge creation, translation and transmission at an individual and system level. Through design for knowledge we seek to guide behavioural change and reduce risk, with the aim of prevention, clarification and promotion of healthcare issues.

While astonishing advances in medical treatment over the past century have allowed practitioners to better address health issues, many preventable diseases and conditions are still prevalent. Such conditions

---

[1] Inserm, "Health Education for Young People: Approaches and Methods," *INSERM Collective Expert Reports*, 2000.

© The Author(s) 2020
E. Nusem et al., *Design Innovation for Health and Medicine*,
https://doi.org/10.1007/978-981-15-4362-3_5

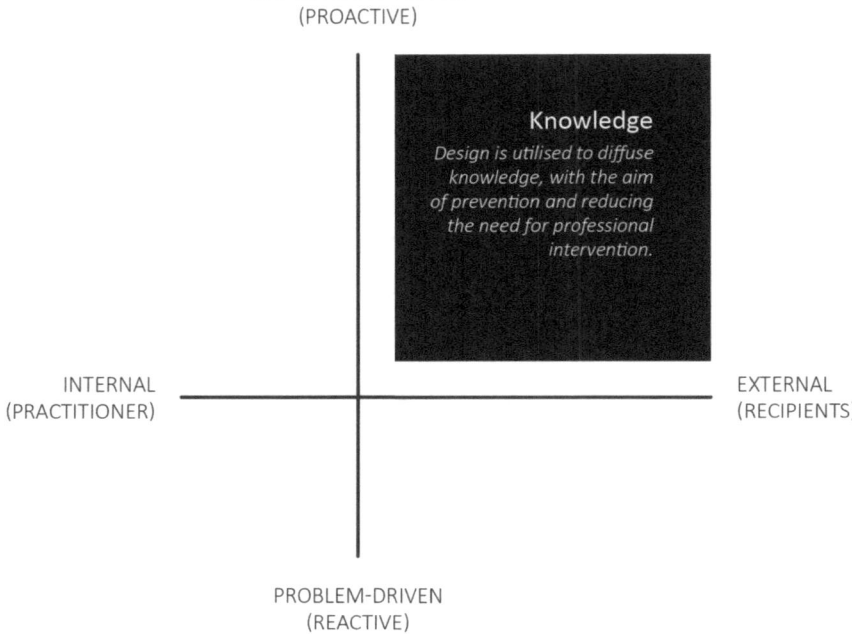

OPPORTUNITY-DRIVEN
(PROACTIVE)

Knowledge

*Design is utilised to diffuse
knowledge, with the aim
of prevention and reducing
the need for professional
intervention.*

INTERNAL
(PRACTITIONER)

EXTERNAL
(RECIPIENTS)

PROBLEM-DRIVEN
(REACTIVE)

Fig. 5.1 Design for knowledge

place an unnecessary burden on our systems, demonstrating the necessity of a proactive approach to care. As articulated by the World Health Organization, health promotion is 'the process of enabling people to increase control over and improve their health'.[2] The Fourth Global Conference on Health Promotion further highlighted the importance of developing prevention and education as an approach to health promotion.[3] Education is not just about identifying which behaviours are risky or which are preventable, but about understanding how people can take

---

[2] Health promotion encompasses social and environmental interventions designed to safeguard and benefit an individual's health and quality of life. The social interventions, in particular, can be considered to be a part of design for knowledge. For more information see World Health Organization, "What Is Health Promotion?," 2016, https://www.who.int/.

[3] Additional information on the conference can be found at "Fourth International Conference on Health Promotion" at https://www.who.int/.

control of their own health—with healthcare practitioners, groups and individuals all taking a role in promoting this agenda.

Many individuals already adopt positive behaviours that are preventative in nature (e.g. physical exercise and nutrition) due to healthcare trends and social conditions, yet often for the sake of pleasure or wellbeing rather than prevention. Building the knowledge of why such practices are needed, through dissemination of best practice and providing access to the right information, can have significant economic outcomes.

Design for knowledge is often opportunity driven and therefore tends to be proactive. Additionally, such innovations are designed with an external frame of view, with a focus on the general public and the recipients of medical services. Disseminating knowledge through design develops greater awareness of medical risks and conditions, with the aim of minimising the need for medical intervention and developing treatment for incurable conditions. A number of design typologies realise this goal. Largely, these designs:

- provide more considered templates for newer designs
- raise awareness and funds to tackle prominent healthcare challenges
- provide relevant and contextual healthcare information to the general public.

The case studies outlined in this chapter will illustrate these points and are segmented across three typologies. First, *blueprints* that assist the healthcare sector to design for more holistic outcomes. Second, through marketing campaigns that seek to raise *awareness* and funds to further explore medical conditions. Finally, through *visual communications* that allow the public to make more informed healthcare decisions. In each of these typologies we describe a number of case studies that exemplify the notion of 'knowledge' (see Table 5.1).

Blueprints

The term 'blueprint' is generally used in reference to a floor plan. In this context, we use the term to infer a plan or guideline that informs more conscious design. These plans guide the design of medical infrastructure, often relating to the design of hospitals and accommodation for the

Table 5.1 Design for knowledge overview

Design for Knowledge	Typology		Case study
Design is utilised to increase public health knowledge, with the aim of prevention and reducing the need for medical intervention	Blueprints	Assist designers in the healthcare sector to design more holistic outcomes	Thrive Project Hospitable hospice
	Awareness	Marketing campaigns that seek to raise awareness and funds to further explore medical conditions	Ice Bucket Challenge World's Greatest Shave
	Visual communication	Contextually dispersed to allow the public to make more informed health and medicine decisions	Packaging pills Rescue Rashie

elderly. Two case studies that relate to these dimensions are explored in the following sections.

Thrive Project: Perceptions of Hospitals

The experience of a patient's hospital stay is a core influence on their overall emotional and mental health. Presenting a calm and supportive environment for patients is a critical component of healthcare services.[4] This example details the use of positive psychology, education and wellness to change perceptions of a hospital stay.

The Florida Hospital for Children launched the Thrive Project to create an interactive and fun environment for both staff and patients. As Thrive Consulting describes,[5] designers were employed to focus on 'empathizing with patients and staff' with the aim of providing a happier and healthier hospital experience. Under this brief, they created an

[4] Cláudia Campos Andrade and Ann Sloan Devlin, "Stress Reduction in the Hospital Room: Applying Ulrich's Theory of Supportive Design," *Journal of Environmental Psychology* 41 (2015): 125–34.

[5] For more information on the Florida Hospital for Children Thrive project, see "Florida Hospital Uses Human-Centered Design" at https://thrivethinking.com/.

interactive, fun and homely environment. The use of ambient lights and sound technologies sought to help children to disconnect from their circumstances and feel more 'child-like' and carefree. The floor plan was co-designed with the primary stakeholders (patients, clinicians and families), giving the stakeholders a voice, and providing transparency over the process.

Various design disciplines were used through the project, including architecture, interior design, product design, experience design and systems design. Collectively, these disciplines changed the way people, especially children, perceived the hospital environment and shared knowledge, by promoting togetherness (see Note 5). As technology continues to advance and shape the way people interact with one another, we must also consider how these advances affect hospital systems. For example, Thrive's 'blueprint' could be used as a guideline for children's hospitals around the world, mapping back to current issues associated with the hospital environment.

Hospitable Hospice: Redefining End-of-Life Care

A hospice is a place of care for people who are terminally ill, where their practical and emotional needs are dealt with alongside their medical needs. Understandably, there is significant social stigma towards hospices. This is largely a result of the discomfort associated with end of life and what it means to have a 'good death'. As a result, little is known about how such environments can be designed to deliver optimal care and an uplifting experience.

The Lien Foundation in Singapore sought to address this through an engagement with the design consultancy fuelfor, which was commissioned to redesign the experience of death and dying, not only in Singapore but also worldwide[6]—an ambitious goal given the global differences in cultures and healthcare systems. The initial challenge faced by fuelfor was understanding how stakeholders (patients, caregivers, family and staff members) interacted with one another in hospices. This process

---

[6] Lekshmy Parameswaran and László Herczeg, "Hospitable Hospice-Redesigning Care for Tomorrow," in International Journal of Integrated Care, vol. 16, 2016, 1–8.

took nine months as the design team engaged with key stakeholders and co-designed their future. Key questions included understanding all stakeholders' needs, values, hopes and fears for end-of-life care, and how these insights could inform the hospice care experience and create a blueprint to guide future care facilities.[7]

The output of this process was a freely available handbook that presents seven key concepts to improve the overall experience for patients, caregivers, family and staff members.[8] These concepts are underpinned by 24 universal experience design principles that act as building blocks for creating future services and spaces within hospitable hospices. The handbook serves as a blueprint for other designers or project managers to implement across hospices globally. By making the design open source, the knowledge in this blueprint offers a significant social contribution.

Knowledge Through Blueprints

As outlined in these cases, by designing blueprints or by making contextual research findings open access (free to the public) we are able to share knowledge and achieve greater impact for our healthcare communities. Such designs do much to improve quality of life for patients, but require organisations to forgo concerns surrounding intellectual property and revenue.

Awareness

Awareness of challenges in health and medicine plays a large role in our society's ability to mitigate medical conditions. While many afflictions are curable, or have procedures for patients to cope with and manage their condition, there remain a large number of ailments that remain untreatable. In this context, designing for awareness can bring such conditions into public focus, generally with the aim of raising funds in the search for treatment. We illustrate awareness through two examples: the Ice Bucket Challenge and World's Greatest Shave.

---

[7] Parameswaran and Herczeg, "Hospitable Hospice-Redesigning Care for Tomorrow."

[8] For more information on the handbook, see fuelfor Healthcare Innovation, *Hospitable Hospice Redesigning Care for Tomorrow*, 2003, https://issuu.com/fuelfor.

Ice Bucket Challenge: Power of People

The Ice Bucket Challenge (see Fig. 5.2 for an illustrative example) was created to promote awareness and disseminate knowledge of the incurable disease Amyotrophic Lateral Sclerosis (also known as Motor Neurone Disease). The challenge became a global phenomenon, with individuals being nominated by their peers to film themselves tipping a bucket of ice water over their head, nominating three others to do the same over social media platforms, and making a donation for research on the disease.[9] Part of the Ice Bucket Challenge's success can be attributed to the use of social media to engage a wide variety of audiences, including celebrity

Fig. 5.2 How the Ice Bucket Challenge works

[9] Michael P. Schlaile, Theresa Knausberg, Matthias Mueller, and Johannes Zeman. "Viral Ice Buckets: A Memetic Perspective on the ALS Ice Bucket Challenge's Diffusion." *Cognitive Systems Research* 52 (2018): 947–69.

involvement, which snowballed into other high-profile engagement (e.g. Oprah Winfrey, Bill Gates, Steven Spielberg and Martha Stewart).

During the first Ice Bucket Challenge, the eight-week campaign raised US$115 million,[10] compared to the US$64 million raised by the ALS Association in the entirety of the previous year.[11] Through social media this experience was able to go viral, enabling participants and nominees to organically act as recruiters through the design of a novel interaction. The global community was therefore seen as the entity driving engagement, rather than the organisation or institution. Design played an important role in the overall development of the Ice Bucket Challenge campaign, by providing an understanding of what would motivate people to become involved in the challenge.

World's Greatest Shave: Inclusion Through Empathy

Despite being launched over 20 years ago, the World's Greatest Shave is still one of the highest grossing campaigns in Australia for cancer awareness. The campaign raises awareness for leukaemia, which is a cancer of the blood that affects more than 13,000 Australians every year.[12] The Leukaemia Foundation developed the World's Greatest Shave—a global campaign that involves people shaving or dyeing their hair—to promote awareness of, disseminate knowledge about, and raise money for research into blood cancer.[13] The campaign is a source of much-needed funding for research into the disease, leveraging social media across a broad range of platforms to reach its audience.

Personalised and direct marketing has allowed people on a global stage to feel engaged with the campaign through donations, participation or both. Specifically, the experience surrounding the campaign has been

---

[10] For information on the capital raised through the Ice Bucket Challenge along with what it funded see "Progress Since the Ice Bucket Challenge" at http://www.alsa.org/.

[11] For more information on the success of the Ice Bucket Challenge relative to previous initiatives see "Ice Bucket Challenge Nears $80-Million Mark" at https://time.com/.

[12] For extra background on the campaign see Nicole Economos, "The World's Greatest Shave Gender Balance Is Equal for the First Time," Sydney Morning Herald, 2018.

[13] The official campaign website is at by the Leukaemia Foundation can be found at https://worldsgreatestshave.com/.

designed so that those who participate are able to feel special, and their local networks feel as though the campaign is personalised. This allows donations to be more intrinsic, and therefore more forthcoming than donations made to a random individual or an institution. Furthermore, participants and their networks are organically recruited through the campaign to aid in sourcing donors.

Knowledge Through Awareness

Engaging with the wider population surrounding charity work can be a difficult task. It requires standing out and being memorable. Having an incentive that makes people want to share their experience with others requires careful planning and design. The two campaigns detailed in this typology have demonstrated how unique, engaging interactions can be used to develop awareness in health and medicine.

Visual Communication

The design of visual communication is pivotal in ensuring that we are able to effectively use the information available to us. Effective communication is often as simple as the hand-washing posters that we encounter in bathrooms, or the instructions we follow to open a pill bottle. Simple visual design can have immense outcomes.

Packaging Pills: Tracking Intake

The design of the pill bottle can be traced back to the conception of prescription drugs. Initial designs took the form of cylindrical glass bottles, before evolving into an orange plastic container in the 1950s and incorporating a safety cap in the 1970s.[14] One of the earlier innovations in pill packaging was developed for birth control pills in 1964, featuring patented disc-shaped packaging for scheduling and tracking dosage. This innovation

---

[14] Diane Wendt and Mallory Warner, "Packaging the Pill," National Museum of American History, 2015, https://americanhistory.si.edu/.

was designed by a husband and wife team, Doris and David Wagner, when Doris lost track of whether she had taken her daily pill.[15] The packaging was designed to be shaped like a lady's cosmetics compact so it was discreet and could easily blend into the contents of a woman's handbag. In addition, the movable central dial allowed the user to reveal each pill along the circular plastic container incrementally and thus allowed for easy tracking.

The next major innovation in pill packaging didn't take place until 41 years later. The designer, Deborah Adler, identified several problems with existing pill bottles when her grandmother misunderstood the labelling on a pill bottle and took the wrong dosage.[16] Deborah fundamentally overhauled the visual communication design of the pill bottle with her design of ClearRx (see Fig. 5.3). The 'D-shaped' bottle was designed to allow for a larger label to be placed on the flat surface, with the cap

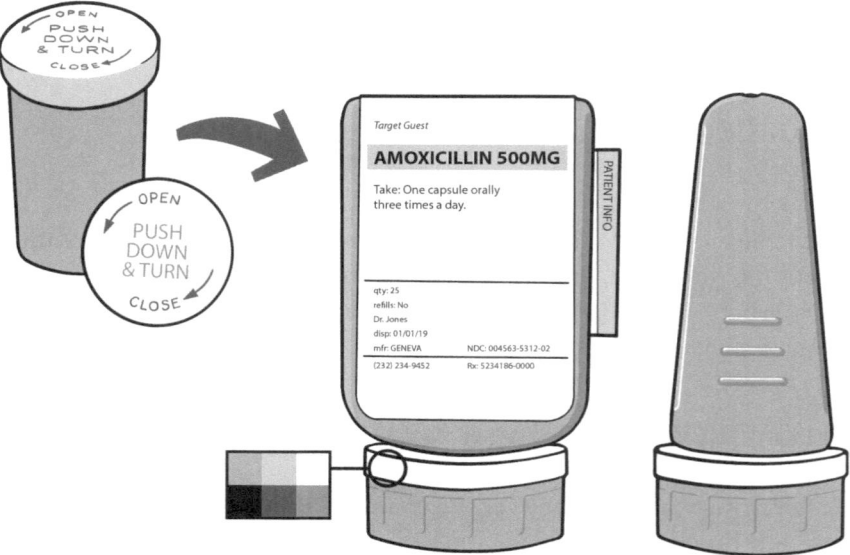

Fig. 5.3 Traditional pill bottle (left) and ClearRx bottle (right)

[15] Patricia Peck Gossel, "Packaging the Pill," in *Manifesting Medicine*, ed. Robert Bud, Bernard Finn, and Helmuth Trischler (London: NMSI Trading Ltd, Science Museum, 1999), 105–21.

[16] Deborah Adler's portfolio and more information on the ClearRX packaging design can be found at https://adlerdesign.com/.

placed on the bottom instead of the top. Six coloured rubber rings were also designed to be attached to the bottle, allowing for a personalised system to ensure family members would not take each other's medication. Instructional and warning graphics were ordered according to an information hierarchy. Target bought ClearRx and launched it in 2005, immediately seeing an increase in their pharmacy sales.[17]

The evolution of pill packaging has been driven by the needs of consumers, from tracking pills to ensuring the correct dosage of medicine. The use of design in this case has addressed the functional requirements of users through a blend of visual and product design to reinforce their knowledge and awareness of their prescription regimens.

Rescue Rashie: Instructions Where They Are Needed

A rashie (also known as a rash guard or rash vest) is an athletic shirt made of a combination of spandex, nylon or polyester. As indicated by its name, the rashie was designed to protect its wearer from rashes caused by abrasion, and from sunburn caused by extended exposure to the sun.[18] Rashies have been around since the early 1950s and have evolved alongside fashion trends, material advancements and manufacturing improvements—with the garments' quality, fashion and function also evolving alongside these developments.

The rashie's function has changed since its inception to include sun protection, especially in Australia. It wasn't until Anzac Day in 2017, when the record of children drowning reached a terrifying high, that companies Westpac and CPR Kids saw the opportunity to help. This led to the development of the Rescue Rashie (see Fig. 5.4).[19]

The Rescue Rashie aims to provide clear guidance to people in situations that are often chaotic and stressful, for example when a child is pulled from water and is suffering from respiratory impairment as a result of being under water. Guidance in this scenario is achieved through the

---

[17] "A Clear Winner: Target Pharmacy's ClearRx Just Got Even Better," 2012, https://corporate.target.com/.

[18] For more information on the history of the rash vest, see Vivien Mitchell, "Brief History of the Rashie," Solar Bare, 2016, https://solarbare.com.au/.

[19] For more information on the Rescue Rashie see the official website at https://www.rescuerashie.com.au/.

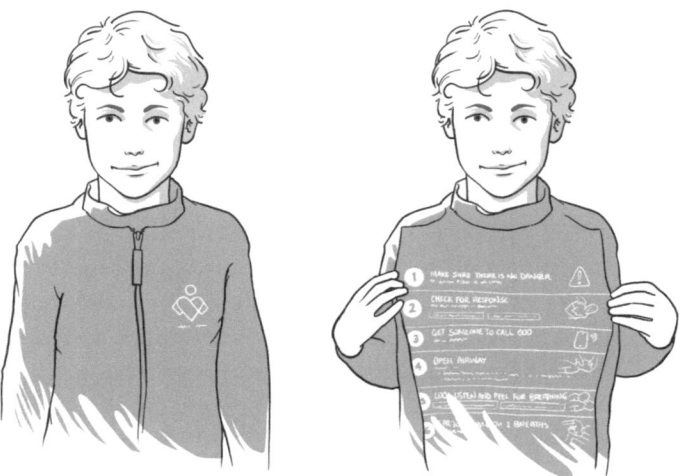

Fig. 5.4   Rescue Rashie

graphic design of simple and easy-to-understand instructions for performing CPR printed on the front side of the rashie with sublimation printing (so the instructions will not fade from the powerful UV rays in Australia).

A number of crucial stakeholders were considered in the product design of the Rescue Rashie, which was developed to not only protect children from harmful UV rays, but also to disseminate knowledge required to save lives. The Rescue Rashie has been developed primarily for children between the ages of two and eight years old. The primary stakeholders in this instance are parents or adults for which the CPR instructions have been designed. Through the use of product and graphic design, the Rescue Rashie is able to offer a simple solution to a prominent social issue.

Knowledge Through Visual Communication

The communication of medical instructions or information is a critical aspect of healthcare; it has tremendous impact when properly executed and dire consequences when integrated poorly. The case studies detailed in this typology are heavily reliant on the first order of design, specifically graphic design. Visual communication can have incredible applications and, while generally cheap and seemingly simple, can be quite difficult to masterfully implement. When done right, graphic design accomplishes much in disseminating knowledge accurately and clearly.

Summarising Design for Knowledge

This chapter explored the role of design in building knowledge within the healthcare sector and wider society. We outlined three types of designs that assist in realising this outcome: blueprints, awareness and visual communication. Through these typologies we explored how the four orders of design are being used to:

- assist in the dissemination of knowledge
- provide more considered templates for designs
- raise awareness and funds to tackle prominent healthcare challenges
- provide relevant and contextual healthcare information to the general public.

Through these outcomes we assist patients to take control of their own health, which:

- reduces strain on healthcare systems
- provides time for practitioners to focus on medical conditions that are not preventable.

Design for knowledge is challenging, as it often necessitates designing for a range of stakeholders (some of which are unknown) rather than a specific user. Furthermore, the success of such designs is often contingent on how easily they can be interpreted or whether they are able to garner adequate support from the general public. Consequently, design should focus on being accessible and on clearly communicating the value created through the design. Table 5.2 describes the four orders of design in this typology, providing a list of considerations and constraints for those seeking to design for knowledge.

Table 5.2 Design for knowledge considerations and constraints

Order	Description	Considerations	Constraints
(1) Graphic design	Graphic design for knowledge is concerned with how information can be shared. As shown in the visual communication typology, through graphic design everyday objects can instil valuable knowledge. The successful use of graphic design can make something standout and interpretable—providing much-needed information in critical moments	• Display of text should be logical and hierarchical in importance • Use of colour, symbols and visuals to allow viewer to quickly identify and interpret information • Style should be consistent with existing standards and norms • Information conveyed should be simple and legible	• Branding, legal and regulatory requirements • Powerful visuals draw attention, but can also distract from the message being conveyed
(2) Industrial design	Industrial design for knowledge is not discussed in depth within our case studies. However, objects such as information terminals in hospitals serve a pivotal role in acting as vessels for knowledge. Other, subtler cues in objects (such as grooves to indicate the placement for fingers on medical devices) can also impart information to users	• Norms and ways of using objects differ across sociocultural contexts • Low-quality products may not elicit trust, acting as a barrier for imparting knowledge • Standalone physical cues in objects may be insufficient for instructing users in methods of use	• Balancing space for explicit (e.g. written text) and implicit (e.g. handhold shape) cues • Information conveyed must be intuitive

(3) Interaction design	Interaction design for knowledge is a means of generating engagement and creating awareness for events (such as fundraising campaigns to combat disease). Such design is concerned with how people can be motivated to become involved and engaged. Inclusion and involvement are integral to these interactions, and require a plan of engagement that details the purpose of the campaign, who should be involved (e.g. celebrities to become 'influencers') and metrics for success	• Appropriate platform(s) for interaction in terms of shareability and dissemination of information • Key stakeholders required to be engaged for successful outcomes • Effective interactions are not designed and deployed *for* people, but *with* people • Question which stakeholder's needs the design should reflect (e.g. patients, staff, regulatory bodies, etc.)	• A layperson should be capable of explaining the interaction (as they are often responsible for disseminating knowledge) • Integration with previous and existing campaigns
(4) System design	The concept of system design for knowledge has not been thoroughly explored in our selected case studies. However, such systems are often used to educate, and to disseminate new standards or practices. These systems serve as the backbone for other modes of design (e.g. through the provision of channels for capturing raised funds or reaching new audiences)	• Accommodating geographical and cultural context of design • Potential for collaborations between education and practice • Understanding how knowledge from completed projects can be disseminated	• Prevalent social trends and concerns • Long-term effectiveness of system and mechanisms employed to disseminate knowledge

6

Design for Enablement

Enablement: To Make Possible

Design for Enablement (see Fig. 6.1) is focused on the enablement of internal stakeholders through the design of 'products' for both health and medicine, to be used in the delivery of medical services. Examples include medical devices such as surgical or diagnostic tools that assist in treating patients.

Design for enablement is often problem-driven and therefore tends to be reactive. Additionally, such designs are developed with an internal frame of view, with a focus on medical practitioners and professionals. Through enablement we ensure that the healthcare sector is properly equipped to tackle challenges in health and medicine. A number of design typologies realise this goal, providing medical professionals the tools required to perform medical procedures, and to capture data to inform decision making. The case studies outlined in this chapter will illustrate these points and showcase how each of the orders of design have been used to assist with enablement.

We segment this chapter across two typologies. First, through *procedural instruments* that assist medical practitioners to perform a range of medical and surgical tasks. Second, through *diagnostic equipment* that assists medical practitioners to make evidence-based decisions. For each

© The Author(s) 2020
E. Nusem et al., *Design Innovation for Health and Medicine*,
https://doi.org/10.1007/978-981-15-4362-3_6

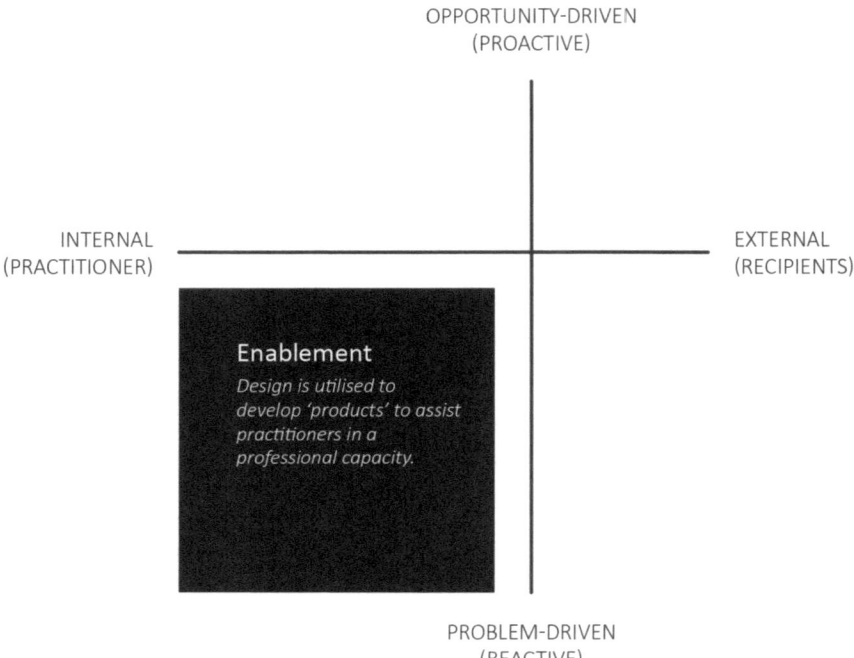

Fig. 6.1   Design for enablement

Table 6.1   Design for enablement overview

Design for enablement	Typology		Case study
Design is utilised to develop 'products' to assist practitioners in a professional capacity	Procedural instruments	A design to assist medical practitioners in performing surgical procedures	Trocar 3D printing Pap smear speculum
	Diagnostics	A design to assist medical practitioners to make evidence-based decisions	Wong-Baker Pain Scale Stethoscope Ultrasound machine

of these typologies we provide a number of case studies that illustrate the notion of 'enablement'. Table 6.1 provides a summary of the typologies and case studies discussed in this chapter.

Procedural Instruments

Medical practices have evolved significantly over the last few decades. This evolution is partly due to our increasing understanding of the human body, but is most significantly marked by the tools and practices that have been developed to assist practitioners with medical procedures. These tools allow us to venture into ever-more complex surgeries and procedures while also minimising the risks to patients. The first typology, procedural instruments, includes three case studies: the trocar, 3D printing for customisation and training and the Pap smear speculum. These cases illustrate how design has influenced and enabled healthcare practitioners in their day-to-day activities.

Trocar: Not Just About Function

The trocar is a surgical instrument: a three-sided cutting point tool, made up of an obturator, a cannula and a seal, that was originally developed to relieve the pressure build-up of fluid or gases in the human body, and is now also used to provide an access port during surgery.[1] The trocar has been innovated many times over the years, with various trocar designs existing today. These designs range in features, size (length and diameter) and the style of tip (single-use and reusable). The original three-point design (for which it was named) is now but one of the several different types available, with flat-bladed and blade-free variants on the market for specific applications. As Belsley[2] describes, the trocar has also changed to a pen-like shape for a more user-friendly and familiar feel, with a single triangular point at one end to allow for accurate and effective piercing of the skin—thus enabling surgeons to improve patient safety. Another advancement is the inclusion of transparent plastic, which enables surgeons to better gauge the trocar's progress through the patient's soft tissues. Developments like these, however, have resulted in high costs.

---

[1] For background explanations on laparoscopic surgery, see Scott Belsley, "What Is Laparoscopic Surgery?," n.d., https://www.laparoscopic.md/.

[2] For more information in the trocar, see Scott Belsey, "Laparoscopic Trocar", n.d., https://www.laparoscopic.md/.

Refinements to the trocar and surgical techniques have helped create safer and more efficient surgical practices. Despite the trocar's long history, there are still a number of functional complications associated with the device. For example, trocar insertion can perforate an underlying organ, resulting in medical complications.

There is constant pressure to reduce costs in healthcare practices, with consumable products being a high-cost area that has continued to receive attention. Trocars, for instance, are often fully or partially disposable, resulting in high costs and waste. Medical company Surgical Innovations understood these issues and designed the YelloPort Elite (see Fig. 6.2) to overcome them.[3] The company created the concept of 'resposable' products: the majority of the trocar is reusable, with only one key component being disposable. The design of the port allows for a range of trocar tips and sizes to be used, featuring a universal seal that enables surgeons to easily change instruments. The redesign of the port has also reduced tissue trauma during removal, which was a key area of concern and infection post operation. This case study is an excellent example of the scope of considerations that exist for products as seemingly simple as the trocar, ranging from issues of use to ethical and cost considerations surrounding the product life cycle.

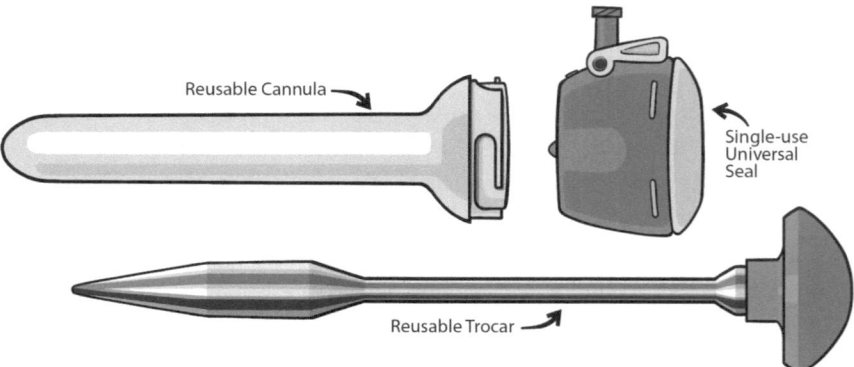

Fig. 6.2   YelloPort Elite

[3] More detail on the YelloPort Elite by Surgical Innovations can be found at https://www. surginno.com/.

3D Printing: Customised Solution to Assistive Tools

After the removal of a cancer-affected sternum, doctors replaced the rib-cage of a seventeen-year-old female using an off-the-shelf solution.[4] While the cancer removal was successful, the sternum is a particularly tricky part of the chest to reconstruct due to the complex shape and the need for the chest cavity to expand and contract when breathing.[5] Unfortunately, the replaced ribcage left the patient with ongoing pain and breathing problems. The solution to this challenge was a patient-specific implant design based on the CT scan data of the individual patient. It was 3D printed from titanium and incorporated a unique polyethylene material to encourage integration with the remaining bone (see Note 4). The ability to create customised prosthetics has impacts beyond patient outcomes and experiences; it could also signify the start of new forms of medical businesses. One such Australian business is Lab 22, which has successfully sent 3D printed prosthetics to patients in the USA and Spain (see Note 4).

3D printing has significant advantages over highly specialised, traditional, labour-intensive implant manufacturing processes,[6] and fits well into traditional design processes of iteration, prototyping and testing. Hospitals are not only creating customised solutions for medical challenges, but also routinely using patient-specific 3D printed bone models for surgical training, planning and rehearsal.[7] Furthermore, some surgeons have begun to use 3D printed patient-specific organ replicas to practise on prior to performing complex operations. Training on a direct copy of a patient's organ has been proven to enable surgeons in creating more effective pre-operative plans compared to conventional 2D images.[8]

---

[4] Details on the surgery and the implant can be found in Ali Green, "American Woman Receives Aussie-Made 3D Printed Implant," CSIROscope, 2017, https://blog.csiro.au/.

[5] José L. Aranda, Marcelo F. Jiménez, María Rodríguez, and Gonzalo Varela, "Tridimensional Titanium-Printed Custom-Made Prosthesis for Sternocostal Reconstruction," *European Journal of Cardio-Thoracic Surgery* 48, no. 4 (2015): e92–94.

[6] Sean Peel and Dominic Eggbeer, "Additively Manufactured Maxillofacial Implants and Guides – Achieving Routine Use," *Rapid Prototyping Journal* 22, no. 1 (2016): 189–99.

[7] Richard Bibb, Dominic Eggbeer, and Abby Paterson, *Medical Modelling: The Application of Advanced Design and Rapid Prototyping Techniques in Medicine: Second Edition, Medical Modelling: The Application of Advanced Design and Rapid Prototyping Techniques in Medicine: Second Edition* (Elsevier Inc., 2015).

[8] Yi Xiong Zheng et al., "3D Printout Models vs. 3D-Rendered Images: Which Is Better for Preoperative Planning?," *Journal of Surgical Education* 73, no. 3 (2016): 518–23.

Pap Smear Speculum: Moving Beyond the Duck Bill

The successful diagnosis and treatment of cervical cancer has been widely attributed to the Pap (Papanicolaou) smear test. The speculum, originally designed by Dr J. Sims in the nineteenth century, allows doctors to take small cell samples of the cervix using a brush or a small spatula.[9]

The speculum, while still maintaining its original design in both function and form,[10] is far from perfect. The original speculums were one size fits all, yet females are not identical, and there is no such thing as an 'average' female. It wasn't until the late twentieth century that company Welch Allyn launched a line of speculums designed to cater to all sizes of women, allowing practitioners to select the most suitable speculum when conducting a Pap smear (see Note 10). The weighted speculum, used in vaginal surgeries, has an attached weight on the speculum allowing it to remain in place without aid, thus leaving both hands free for the doctor. Other developments include an in-built LED light source, and disposable plastic speculums.[11]

Even with these design enhancements the experience of having a Pap smear remains awkward and uncomfortable. For most women the first test can induce significant stress and anxiety, as it can be difficult to know what to expect. Despite being a relatively short procedure lasting only a few minutes, patients still feel tense and embarrassed.

Pap smear speculums have been conceptualised for the treatment of women, yet have long been designed through the perspective of their users (medical practitioners). A recent redesign of the speculum undertaken by Frog Design challenges this notion, with the redesign focusing on the experience of those undergoing the Pap smear. Frog Design's overall aim was to make the Pap smear experience 'relaxing, empathetic, and

---

[9] Background information on speculum sizing can be found via Goodall Wendy McDonald, "Speculum Sizes: 'One Size Does Not Fit All,' Says Your Friendly Neighborhood Gynecologist," The Gyneco-(B)Logic, 2017, https://gyneco-blogic.com/.

[10] For more information on the design history of the speculum, see Rose Eveleth, "Why No One Can Design a Better Speculum," The Atlantic, 2014, https://www.theatlantic.com/.

[11] Background on the social history of the speculum can be found via Johanna Gohmann, "The Secret History Of The Speculum," Bust Magazine, 2015, https://bust.com/.

even light-hearted'.[12] The female design team looked at the whole experience of a pelvic examination, including pre-, during and post-examination. Their design now incorporates a mobile application that allows patients to privately learn about the procedure beforehand, along with the optional purchase of a comfort kit (socks, weighted blanket, stress ball) to lower anxiety. The exam room has been reconsidered, with the inclusion of a hanger for patients' clothing. A playful graphic that illustrates where a patient should lay on the examination bed was also developed, as Frog Design found that many women felt awkward when asked to move once on the bed. After the examination, the mobile application congratulates the patient on taking care of themselves and provides details of when their examination results should be expected. The material and ergonomics of the speculum were two simple fixes to improve patients' experience during the procedure. The Yona Speculum (see Fig. 6.3) offers a greater balance between clinical needs and patient comfort. In place of the original two-bladed 'duck bill' design, the new design features three blades that open in a triangular shape, reducing the amount the instrument has to open. The silicone-covered metal lessens the mechanical noise and is angled at 110 degrees instead of 90 degrees, which enables the doctor to manipulate the device and their view more comfortably.

Perhaps the most notable redesign in the speculum to date has been in the change from stainless steel to plastic. This change in materials addresses one of the most significant issues faced by users, replacing the traditionally clinical and cold instrument with a light and transparent plastic model. Many doctors and engineers believe the overall shape of the current speculum does not need to be altered as the design is simple and effective (see Note 10). Yet the fear of undergoing a Pap smear still remains, so there is significant potential for future improvements that continue to enable the clinician to obtain appropriate access, while improving the patient's experience.

---

[12] For details on modern speculum designs, see Arielle Pardes, "The Speculum Finally Gets a Modern Redesign," Wired, 2017, https://www.wired.com/.

Fig. 6.3 Yona Speculum

Procedural Instruments for Enablement

The three procedural instrument case studies illustrate the importance of not developing medical devices solely for improved usability, but to also consider how the patient's overall experience can be improved. When selecting cases for this typology we endeavoured to focus on advancements that go beyond materials, technology and manufacturing processes. The examples demonstrate the host of considerations in the design of procedural instruments, from ethical considerations regarding surgical waste to minimising the psychological impacts of medical procedures through the choice of materials in medical instruments (e.g. a plastic speculum in place of a metal one). Even when designing medical instruments to enable a medical practitioner, the patient must not be left out of the equation. The smallest change in the design of a device can have a tremendous impact on outcomes for patients (especially in relation to experiential outcomes). It is also important to consider the implementation of new technologies, such as 3D printing, that can revolutionise practice (e.g. through the customisation of tools and how we prepare for surgery).

Diagnostics

A medical practitioner's ability to make an accurate and evidence-based decision depends on their ability to reliably get the information required to make such decisions. A host of tools and devices have been designed over the years to assist in these endeavours, allowing medical professionals to gather information and optimise patient outcomes. Three case studies are explored in this typology: the Wong-Baker Pain Scale, the U Scope and ultrasound machines.

Wong-Baker FACES Pain Rating Scale: Giving Pain a Face

The Wong-Baker Pain Scale (see Fig. 6.4) was developed in the 1980s by Dr Wong and Connie Baker in order to better gauge children's pain thresholds within the hospital environment.[13] The duo observed that many pain scales were based around numerical values, which were ineffective for patients seeking to communicate how much pain they were experiencing.

The pain scale consists of six different levels of pain that are visually represented by facial expressions.[14] Through these facial expressions patients can more accurately rate and convey their pain level, enabling

Fig. 6.4 Wong-Baker FACES Pain Rating Scale

---

[13] For the history of the Wong-Baker scale, see Connie Baker, "Wong-Baker FACES® History," Wong-Baker FACES Foundation, n.d., https://wongbakerfaces.org/.

[14] Information on the use of the scale can be found via Connie Baker, "Instructions for Use," Wong-Baker FACES Foundation, n.d., https://wongbakerfaces.org/.

medical staff to treat them accordingly. While the pain scale was originally developed for children, it has been adopted globally due to its effectiveness and efficiency. Indeed, patients find that the graphic facial expressions easily correlate to the level of pain they are experiencing. While the scale is effective, it cannot protect against patients lying about the degree of pain they are experiencing in order to receive more immediate attention. There is also potential for digitising the pain scale and incorporating animations, which could assist in making the expressions more relatable. Younger generations, which are more technologically inclined, could also find a digital scale to be more engaging than a more traditional 2D graphic.

U Scope: Modernising a Symbol of Healthcare

Stethoscopes are frequently used to depict doctors in illustrations and media—and are oftentimes regarded as the symbol of healthcare. The first stethoscope was conceptualised by Rene Laennec in 1816, following the use of a rolled piece of paper to amplify sound and assist in hearing the heart of a woman suffering from heart disease.[15] Little has changed in the stethoscope since the nineteenth century beyond minor design alterations, with the underlying concept remaining largely the same. The original design has, however, led to a range of stethoscopes for various purposes, including the acoustic stethoscope, electronic stethoscope and fetal stethoscope—all designed to cater for a specific purpose or patient.

One stethoscope of note is the U scope[16] designed by Yoshio Goodrich Design in 2016 (see Fig. 6.5), which has focused on the device's usability from a practitioner's perspective by tackling the issues of ear aches and neck pain emerging from use. The U scope is designed to fit and balance in the hand, removing the need to think about the grip, while the T-shape structure reduces pressure on the ears. This new shape also allows the device to fold and fit into a pocket. In addition, the design of the packag-

---

[15] Ariel Roguin, "Rene Theophile Hyacinthe Laënnec (1781–1826): The Man behind the Stethoscope," *Clinical Medicine and Research* 4, no. 3 (2006): 230–35.

[16] Information on the U Scope can be found at "U Scope / Stethoscope" at https://ifworlddesignguide.com/.

Fig. 6.5   U scope

ing and option for personalisation through engraving makes it feel less like a medical instrument and more like a premium luxury product (such as something from Apple). The original stethoscope was developed to better understand the human body, while the U scope was also designed to enable the doctor to work more comfortably and efficiently.

Ultrasound Machines: Where and When You Need a Diagnosis

Ultrasound machines were developed to examine organs and structures inside a body by reflecting high-frequency sound waves.[17] First introduced at the Royal Hospital for Women with the 'Mk I Abdominal Echoscope' in the early 1960s, the machine was primarily used to develop a better understanding of the various stages of pregnancy.[18] Ultrasound machines have been a significant innovation in the medical industry,

---

[17] For more information on ultrasound, see Yolanda Smith, "What Is an Ultrasound?," News-Medical, 2018, https://www.news-medical.net/.

[18] Additional information on the history of ultrasound can be found at "History of Medical Ultrasound" at http://www.asum.com.au/.

offering a non-destructive and cost-effective way for visualising issues internal to the human body. Applications of modern ultrasound machines have expanded to producing images that assist in diagnosing a range of conditions, including cancer, liver and gallbladder functions, and joint inflammation.[19] Over the years, ultrasound machines have not only changed in their applications, but also in aesthetics and experience of use.

Medical manufacturer Philips[20] has pioneered many of the advances in ultrasound machines, from alterations to how medical practitioners interact with the machine to a more user friendly, ergonomic and simplistic design. Historically, a significant limitation of the ultrasound machine has been its lack of portability. The original ultrasound scanners were large and immobile, which resulted in numerous challenges for medical staff. In 1984 Philips developed a mobile console that could be easily manoeuvred around the patient.[21] This design was a response to challenges articulated by staff regarding mobility, with new technologies from existing products being adapted to improve usability.[22]

Even with these product developments, ultrasound machines are still designed for use within a hospital context, with portability limitations. Building on their original innovation, Philips has addressed this concern with the development of Lumify (see Fig. 6.6), a tele-ultrasound that uses a mobile application and plug-in transducer for a truly portable ultrasound scanner. The scanner provides the ability to share images and videos in real time, enabling use in a range of new situations, such as during emergencies (e.g. in ambulances and care units), in rural locations, in bedside assessment and in smaller GP practices.

---

[19] To learn about ultrasound procedures, see Mayo Clinic, "Ultrasound," 2018, https://www.mayoclinic.org/.

[20] Details about Philips ultrasound machines can be found via "Ultrasound Machines and Software" at https://www.philips.com/.

[21] Paola Bertola and Jose Carlos Teixeira, "Design as a Knowledge Agent: How Design as a Knowledge Process Is Embedded into Organizations to Foster Innovation," *Design Studies* 24, no. 2 (2003): 181–94.

[22] Erez Nusem, "Design in Healthcare: Challenges and Opportunities," in *Design Research Society Conference 2018 "Catalyst"* (Limerick, Ireland, 2018), 2380–89.

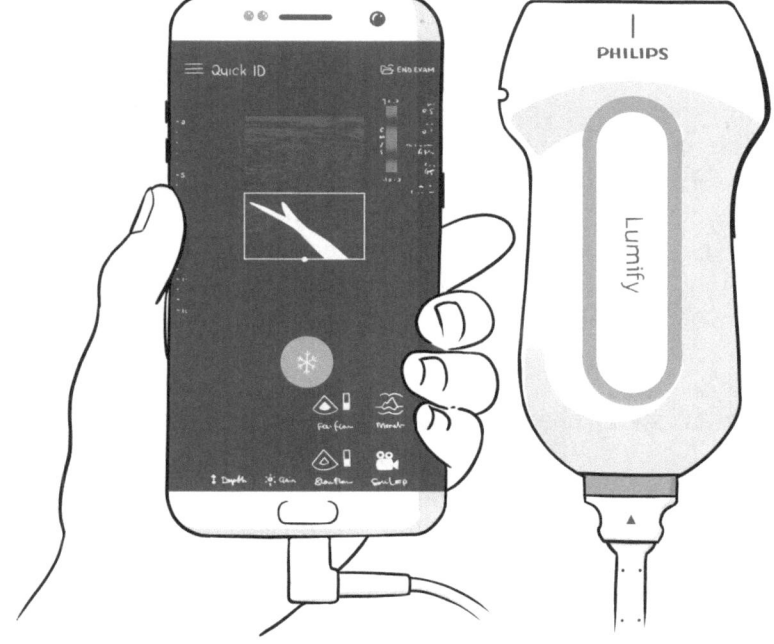

Fig. 6.6 Lumify

Diagnostics for Enablement

Designing diagnostic equipment that medical practitioners use to make evidence-based decisions is considered to be in the remit of engineering. An engineer typically develops a solution for a clinical problem that is more efficient or effective than the current paradigm. As seen in the conceptualisation of the original stethoscope, designers are often not considered as part of the process. For many innovations, medical practitioners liaise directly with engineers to realise their visions. However, this results in a tendency for the focus of development to lie solely on the outcome, rather than the experience of using such inventions. The U scope case study highlights the skill set of product designers, who practise the second order of design and are trained to holistically approach all facets of use in their designs. In turn, this enables medical practitioners to perform their duties to the best of their abilities, translating into better patient outcomes. For example, through designs such as the Wong-Baker Pain

Scale, which assists patients in better communicating the amount of pain they are experiencing.

Diagnostics play an integral element in the healthcare system—but also feature a host of considerations that typically reach beyond diagnosis. These considerations, amongst others, include the aesthetics and usability of established devices (e.g. the work conducted in developing the U scope), or reconsidering the context of use for diagnostic equipment (e.g. the design of the truly portable ultrasound Lumify). Collectively, the three case studies illustrate the variety of roles design plays in enabling diagnosis by medical practitioners in healthcare.

Summarising Design for Enablement

Design for enablement features an internal frame of view, with a focus on medical practitioners and professionals. It is concerned with developing 'products' to assist practitioners in a professional capacity. Two typologies were discussed in design for enablement: procedural instruments and diagnostics. Through these typologies we explored how the four orders of design have been used to assist with enablement by:

- providing the tools required to perform medical procedures
- capturing data to inform decision making.

There are a number of impacts and implications from design for enablement, including:

- optimisation of procedures and processes
- customisation of solutions and assistant tools to reduce surgery time and patient trauma
- faster manufacturing processes
- new possibilities for education and training.

Design for enablement ensures that the healthcare sector is properly equipped to tackle challenges in health and medicine. Table 6.2 describes the four orders of design in this typology, providing examples of considerations and constraints to be considered when designing solutions for enablement.

Table 6.2   Design for enablement considerations and constraints

Order	Description	Considerations	Constraints
(1) Graphic design	A prominent use of graphic design for enablement is to facilitate communication. Visualisations, like those used in the Wong-Baker Pain Scale, enable stakeholders to better communicate through graphics or symbols, and thus overcome language barriers. Visuals can be more inclusive than words, as individuals have different understandings of language, terminology and definitions. Poor visuals, however, can hinder communication between stakeholders	• Modes of communication available between patients and medical practitioners • Options for cross-cultural communication • Different understandings of medical terminology between medical professions (e.g. nurses and doctors) and geographic contexts	• Limited space for graphic components on medical devices • Visuals and text are often an afterthought or not considered at all
(2) Industrial design	Industrial design for enablement generally focuses on aesthetics and functionality. However, the case studies selected in this chapter have demonstrated a host of considerations that are often overlooked or marginalised. Amongst others, these include a product's lifecycle (e.g. trocar) and the experience of patients when interacting with medical devices (e.g. the Yona speculum)	• Better materials and ergonomics could improve the procedural experience for stakeholders • Balance between clinical needs and patient comfort • Established legacy designs • Existing support systems (e.g. for managing waste)	• Requirement of approval process, device registration and listing • Notification requirements for any repair, replacement, and refund on products • Practices, standards and guidelines for manufacturing and products

(continued)

Table 6.2 (continued)

Order	Description	Considerations	Constraints
(3) Interaction design	Interaction design for enablement helps medical practitioners frame the experiences patients have when engaging with medical services and institutions. Specifically, these interactions serve in supporting products by creating positive experiences for patients that enable better medical outcomes	• Alternative contexts and scenarios of use • Ill-considered or overlooked users during medical services • How interactions can best support existing practices	• Technology-driven solutions are often sought over experience-driven solutions
(4) System design	System design for enablement is about establishing appropriate processes and systems to enable medical practitioners to perform medical practices and procedures. Such systems often provide oversight of available tools and future opportunities	• Ability to customise design with use of emerging technology (e.g. 3D printing) • The scalability of new training methods (e.g. application in rural settings)	• Resistance and discomfort to new approaches and practices • Time commitment to developing and understanding new systems

7

Design for Empowerment

Empowerment: Freedom

Despite great the strides made in the treatment of illness, the focus of care is often on quantity (medical outcomes and years lived) rather than quality (experience) of life. In other words, on the disease rather than the person with the disease.[1] This is not a surprise, given that current healthcare systems generally offer symptom-driven care and are designed to provide efficient treatment for acute and immediate issues. Consequently, patients may find that there is insufficient focus on their experience during care and on their overall wellbeing.

Empowering patients to make the right decisions and to manage their treatment is an integral component in the continuum of healthcare. The outcome of empowerment, as discussed in this chapter, is therefore a patient-centred, collaborative approach that tailors healthcare to the individual. Design for empowerment takes into account the patient's priorities, as well as their physiological and psychosocial factors. Empowerment is defined in this context as helping patients discover and develop responsibility for their own health. In the provision of care, it is important to

---

[1] Adrian E. Bauman, John H. Fardy, and Peter G. Harris, "Getting It Right: Why Bother with Patient-Centred Care?," *Medical Journal of Australia* 179, no. 5 (2003): 253–56.

© The Author(s) 2020
E. Nusem et al., *Design Innovation for Health and Medicine*,
https://doi.org/10.1007/978-981-15-4362-3_7

distinguish between how an illness affects a patient's body and mind, and how an illness affects a person's life—as these are fundamentally different aspects. Likewise, it is important to acknowledge that patients are the primary decision-maker and in control of their daily health management, and that healthcare practices should reflect this. Before this philosophy can be embraced, we must first reframe healthcare into practices that empower patients to take charge of their health and wellbeing.

Empowerment is a vision that guides our encounters with patients and the things that we design for them.[2] It requires shifts in patients' and professionals' existing roles, allowing each party to adopt new roles that will result in more holistic, and eventually more effective, care. This would see patients become responsible for keeping themselves informed and active collaborators in their care. Health professionals will be responsible for assisting patients to make informed decisions that will ultimately help them to realise their goals and overcome barriers through education, recommendations, advice and support.[3] With this change, health professionals are able to shift from feeling responsible *for* patients to becoming responsible *to* them. By bringing expertise on illness and treatment, they can work hand in hand with patients as they, in turn, bring expertise on their own lives and what will work for them.

Design for empowerment (see Fig. 7.1) is an ideology centred around the wellbeing of healthcare recipients, evident through examples including the design of hospitable aged care environments,[4] or empowering individuals with disabilities or acute conditions to face adversity (e.g. Cochlear hearing implants for the deaf, or Liftware eating utensils for individuals who experience hand tremors or have limited hand and arm mobility).

Innovations such as these are designed with an external frame of view, focusing on the recipients of care and how this care intercedes with their day-to-day lives, instead of inside the consultation room. These designs aim to empower patients, taking away the burden of whatever condition or illness they and their families must endure.

---

[2] Martha M. Funnell and Robert M. Anderson, "Empowerment and Self-Management of Diabetes," *Clinical Diabetes* 22, no. 3 (2004): 123–27.

[3] Olga Dreeben-Irimia, Patient Education in Rehabilitation (Sudbury, Massachusetts: Jones & Bartlett Publishers, 2010).

[4] Parameswaran and Herczeg, "Hospitable Hospice-Redesigning Care for Tomorrow."

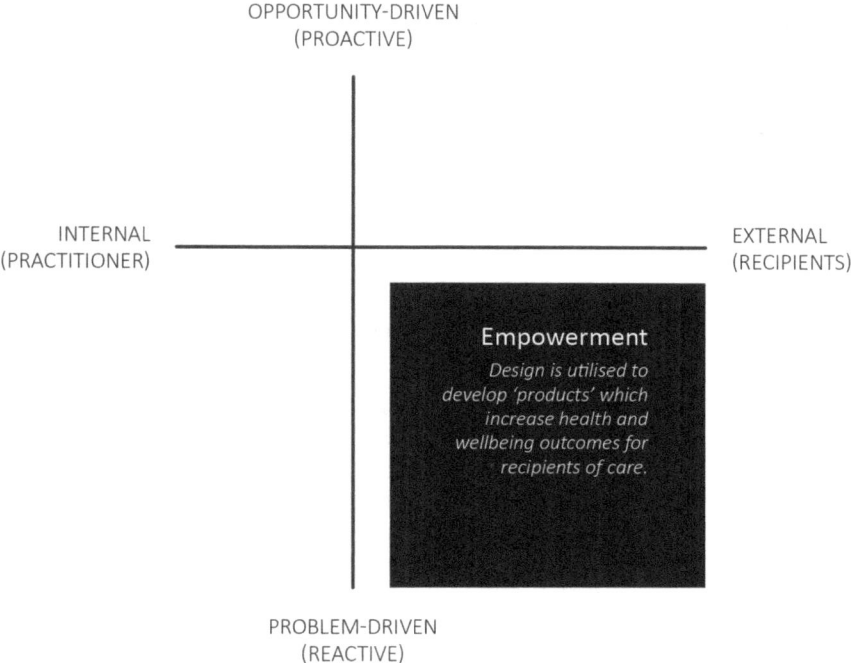

OPPORTUNITY-DRIVEN
(PROACTIVE)

INTERNAL
(PRACTITIONER)

EXTERNAL
(RECIPIENTS)

Empowerment
*Design is utilised to
develop 'products' which
increase health and
wellbeing outcomes for
recipients of care.*

PROBLEM-DRIVEN
(REACTIVE)

Fig. 7.1   Design for empowerment

Design for empowerment can be seen across three typologies. First, through *promoting ability*, secondly through *confidence instillers* and lastly through *experiential design* (see Table 7.1).

Promoting Ability

Many medical conditions impact patients' lifestyles and create challenges in daily life. Fortunately, a multitude of products have been designed to assist individuals with such conditions in minimising and, in some cases, mitigating their challenges. We explore three such products in the typology of *promoting ability*: Liftware, Cochlear and TickleFLEX.

Table 7.1 Design for empowerment overview

Design for empowerment	Typology	Description	Case study
Design is utilised to develop 'products' that increase health and medicine outcomes for recipients of care	Promoting ability	Assist individuals in minimising and, in some cases, negating medical challenges	Liftware Cochlear TickleFLEX
	Confidence instillers	Assist in developing patients' confidence and ability to retain control over their own life	EpiPen Tango Belt
	Experiential design	Empower patients with well-designed experiences that often have other significant outcomes for stakeholders	Tovertafel Original Kitten Scanner SnowWorld Incubator

Liftware: Eating with Stability

Liftware was founded in 2012 by a group of scientists and engineers seeking to develop new products and technologies to aid people suffering from hand tremors and limited hand–arm mobility.[5] The company has developed stabilising and levelling attachments that empower these individuals to eat without aid from others (an extraordinarily difficult feat without specialised utensils). Two of their products, Liftware Steady (for those with hand tremors) and Liftware Level (for those with limited hand and arm mobility, see Fig. 7.2), help their users to accomplish this task. Both products have a battery-operated handle with sensors that detect hand motion and stabilise it by moving in the opposite direction. Interchangeable cutlery attachments are available, so users can choose between spoons and forks.

Liftware presents a simple yet effective application of industrial design. The device leverages technology to address a prevalent challenge, and doesn't rely on other modes of design to help accomplish its purpose.

---

[5] For more information on Liftware and their offerings visit the official site at https://www.liftware.com/.

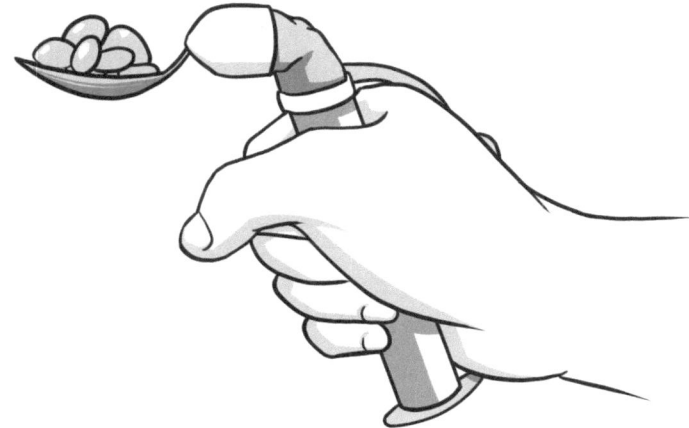

Fig. 7.2   Liftware Level

Cochlear: Ensuring Everyone Can Hear

Cochlear implants (see Fig. 7.3) are medical devices that 'use electronic stimulation and replace the function of the inner ear'.[6] Each implant contains a micro receiver that is placed under the skin behind the user's ear to imitate the function of sensory hair cells within the inner ear. The cochlear implant has evolved over the decades, with the first successfully commercialised multichannel cochlear implant named 'Cochlear/ Nucleus' implanted by otologist Graeme Clark in 1978.[7] Since then Cochlear, both as a company and a product, have come a long way in design, innovation and technological advances. Although the hearing implant has changed in aesthetics and processing, the principle of empowerment has remained the same: to 'help people hear and be heard, through empowering people to connect with others and live a full life'.[8]

---

[6] For details about cochlear implants, visit "How cochlear implants work" at https://www.cochlear.com/.

[7] Albert Mudry and Mara Mills, "The Early History of the Cochlear Implant: A Retrospective," *JAMA Otolaryngology – Head and Neck Surgery* 139, no. 5 (2013): 446–53.

[8] As can be seen in the "About us" section on the organisation's official website https://www.cochlear.com/.

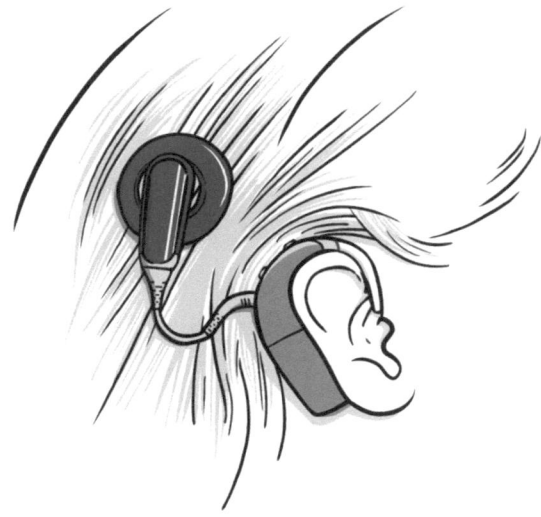

Fig. 7.3 Cochlear implant

Cochlear identified the need to better understand how the human ear works in relation to hearing loss and impairment. Through using the first order of design Cochlear articulated their vision as 'Hear Now. And Always', making their purpose clear and sharing their vision of making everyone able to hear, while focusing on recipients of their products and their families. Their logo, a symbolic representation of an eardrum paired with their slogan, makes their purpose explicit, resulting in their brand being known globally for gifting people with a new way to hear. They have continued to listen to users' desires: they were the first to develop implants that can stream music, phone calls and entertainment directly from smart phones (see Note 5). They have also continued to make their implants smaller and lighter, ensuring they are less intrusive and more comfortable for people to wear. As a company Cochlear offers a lifetime commitment, stating that patients will feel a sense of family from the start of their relationship with them. The Cochlear community provides support with rehabilitation, access to industry experts, and service and repairs.[9]

[9] For additional information see "Cochlear Guiding Principles" at https://www.cochlear.com/.

Following this strategy has allowed Cochlear to maintain their position as market leaders for decades.

Cochlear empowers people to connect with others and live a full life, through transforming the way people understand and treat hearing loss.[10] Cochlear has used design methods to achieve the high standard of product available today, however this would not have been possible without Cochlear's mission to better understand their users.

TickleFLEX: Insulin Injection Aid

Manufacturers have developed and redesigned the insulin needle many times, producing thinner and sharper points that reduce the amount of pressure required for penetration. However, many issues from injections, especially self-injection, do not relate to the needle but to the patient's skin.

Diabetic UK-based engineer Peter Bailey created TickleFLEX,[11] an injection aid that makes self-injection safer, more consistent and comfortable. Key issues that Bailey observed and personally experienced through daily self-injections included hitting nerves, injecting into muscle and simply being unable to reach sites or steadily self-inject.[12] The TickleFLEX is a simple, low-tech solution. The device is slid over a needle and pressed onto the skin, gathering and securing it, which prevents needle shear by providing a steady hold (see Fig. 7.4). The cover also hides the needle entering the skin, and is textured to provide sensory distraction for the user, two known issues that people suffering from needle phobia struggle with. The design allows for consistent injection every time, preventing insulin leakage. The design looks beyond the needle and focuses on the user's experience of self-injection, providing a simple and effective solution that empowers them to manage their own condition reliably.

---

[10] As articulated by Cochlear on their official website https://www.cochlear.com/.

[11] The TickleFLEX official website can be found at https://www.tickleflex.com/.

[12] Information on the history of TickleFLEX can be found on Peter Bailey, "History of TickleFLEX," n.d., https://www.tickleflex.com/.

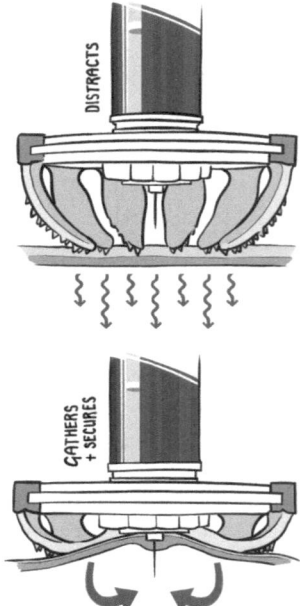

Fig. 7.4 TickleFLEX self-injection process

Empowerment Through Promoting Ability

As shown in these case studies, patients can be empowered to live a relatively normal life with the help of carefully designed medical devices. This is only made possible by adopting a patient-centric approach to design. When such devices and products are researched and designed well, they empower, strengthen and inspire the patient to consider themselves able and competent.

Confidence Instillers

Some medical conditions are severe or intrusive enough that they sap a patient's confidence, and demand patients remain vigilant and prepared at all times. While not necessarily posing a consistent challenge, these conditions can often be acutely detrimental to a patient's mental and emotional, as well as physical, health. Products in this context, illustrated here through the EpiPen and Tango Belt case studies, assist in developing patients' confidence and ability to retain control over their own life.

EpiPen: Simple and Effective Design

EpiPens were developed to treat extreme allergic reactions to insect stings, bites, drugs and nut allergies. EpiPens are portable injectable devices that contain a drug called epinephrine, a chemical that narrows the blood vessels while opening airways to the lungs.[13] The primary aim of the EpiPen is to rapidly medicate a person who is suffering from a serious allergic reaction, sustaining them until they can receive medical care.

In the early 2000s the EpiPen (see Fig. 7.5) was developed by Mylan Pharmaceuticals.[14] Mylan combined various design elements and principles throughout the product development stages. As EpiPens are classified as self-administering medical devices, the design must ensure patients are empowered to safely inject themselves.

The design of the EpiPen has been centred upon its use.[15] An elliptical shape allows for a firm grip and fast retrieval from a bag, and the instructions are located on the pen itself and separated into three simple, easy-to-understand steps supported by words and images. The starkly contrasting colours of blue and orange were selected so that even colour-blind people can orient the needle. A blue safety-release cap was designed to prevent unintentional use, while the orange top aids in quick identification of the needle end. The use of colour also aids in recalling the instructions of 'Blue to the sky. Orange to the thigh'. Once the orange tip has been placed on the thigh, the auto-injector is pushed for three seconds to administer the drug. The 'never-see-needle' function protects against

---

[13] Information on the epinephrine injection can be accessed via Suman Varandani, "What Is EpiPen And What Does It Do? Everything You Need To Know About Epinephrine Injection," Medical Daily, 2016.

[14] EpiPen history can be found via Matt Reimann, "The Story of the EpiPen: From Military Technology to Drug-Industry Cash Cow," Timeline, 2016, https://timeline.com/.

[15] Instructions for use are available at Mylan, "How to Use an EpiPen' (Epinephrine Injection, USP) Auto-Injector," n.d., https://www.epipen.com/.

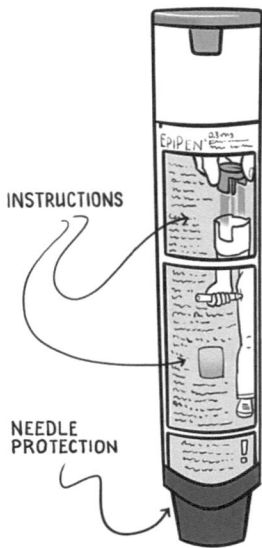

INSTRUCTIONS

NEEDLE
PROTECTION

Fig. 7.5   EpiPen

needle exposure before and after use, and the device has no electronic or battery-operated parts, ensuring it is always ready to be used. This simple solution of an auto-injector is a confidence instiller, as it provides peace of mind for those who fear the fatal effects of anaphylactic shock.

Tango Belt: Reducing the Fear and Impact of Falls

Due to reduced mobility, elderly people living in nursing care facilities are at a higher risk of falling, resulting in hip fractures. Hip protectors are one way to prevent factures and breaks after a fall.[16] They are commonly made from either plastic shields or foam pads that fill a pocket inside specially designed underwear, acting as a protective barrier if a fall occurs. A key issue surrounding hip protectors is noncompliance (hip protectors offer little benefit when not worn). Such noncompliance has been found

---

[16] Nancy Santesso, Alonso Carrasco-Labra, and Romina Brignardello-Petersen, "Hip Protectors for Preventing Hip Fractures in Older People," *Cochrane Database of Systematic Reviews*, no. 3 (2014).

to stem from discomfort, side effects, poor ergonomics (e.g., difficulty of use) and distaste with the aesthetics.[17]

Tango Belt was designed with an understanding of the stigma behind noncompliance and patient requirements within the elderly community. As described by Quigley et al.,[18] the smart belt employs a motion-sensing technology to detect a fall that is likely to result in a hip impact. If a serious hip-impacting fall is sensed, the belt activates an airbag that encompasses the hip to lessen the impact of the fall.

The solution has carefully considered the user experience, reimagining the form of hip protection to combat the stigma associated with device use and increase patient compliance. Elderly people wearing the belt were restored with confidence, empowering them to increase daily mobility.

Empowerment Through Confidence Instillers

Patients can be empowered to live a fulfilling and unconstrained life if their confidence and abilities are restored. The case studies presented in this typology help patients to build confidence in their ability to overcome anaphylactic shock and to move without fear of severe injury from falling. As survival is usually the priority in health and medicine, instilling confidence in patients is often overlooked; however, as this typology shows, instilling confidence can make a huge difference in a patient's life.

Experiential Design

Experience is often a secondary parameter for designs in the context of health and medicine. However, experience is paramount in empowering patients, and a well-considered design often has significant outcomes for other stakeholders in addition to functional efficiency. We explore the vital role of a well-considered design for experience across four case

---

[17] Patricia A. Quigley, Wamis Singhatat, and Rebecca J. Tarbert, "Technology Innovation to Protect Hips from Fall-Related Fracture," *Physical Medicine and Rehabilitation Research* 4, no. 3 (2019): 1–4.

[18] Quigley, Singhatat, and Tarbert, 2.

studies: the Tovertafel dementia games, Philips's Kitten Scanner, SnowWorld and incubators designed for different users and environments.

Tovertafel Dementia Games: A Sense of Connection

There is currently no cure for dementia, so treatments take the form of symptom management. Many dementia sufferers feel isolated and lonely in residential care. Tovertafel Original is a game that empowers elderly people in the late stages of dementia to interact (see Fig. 7.6). It was developed to create moments of happiness in residential care, which often can be places of apathy, disruption or restlessness.[19]

The team behind Tovertafel gained insights into how dementia sufferers and their families felt in residential care through co-design and first-hand observations. These findings informed the development of the Tovertafel Original game, which consists of a ceiling-mounted box that projects a variety of games onto a table or flat surface. The projection is

Fig. 7.6 Original Tovertafel game

[19] Hester Anderiesen, Erik J.A. Scherder, Richard H.M. Goossens, and Marieke H. Sonneveld, "A Systematic Review–Physical Activity in Dementia: The Influence of the Nursing Home Environment," *Applied Ergonomics* 45, no. 6 (2014): 1678–86.

created with the use of various sensors, speakers and processors all working together to generate a physical and cognitive learning environment. The game was specifically designed to stimulate both physical and cognitive functions, thus encouraging social interactions and overcoming the apathy that commonly affects those suffering from dementia.[20] The games produce and stimulate positivity among all those engaging with it, not just those suffering dementia.

Feedback on the game from caregivers and family members includes how positive these interactive and cognitive games are for dementia sufferers. Caregivers even suggest that the games create a calming effect on certain individuals who feel isolated. Through the environment that Tovertafel fosters it is clear that its creators have empathetically identified, addressed and designed for the specific needs of dementia sufferers and their families.

Kitten Scanner: Addressing a Child's Fears and Anxiety

Designers at Philips took a creative approach to designing medical equipment and transformed the way children saw and experienced MRI systems. This was achieved through the Kitten Scanner: an interactive, scaled-down and stylised model of a CT scanner, incorporating a TV screen and several characters including a crocodile, elephant, robot and chicken.[21] While in the waiting room, often an uncomfortable and frightening space, the child can interact with the Kitten Scanner like doctors and nurses would interact with a patient in the real MRI procedure. The child is empowered to place the animal character inside the scanner, which picks up the RFID sensors in the toy, triggering the screen to display a real three-dimensional CAT scan of the toy (see Fig. 7.7). The character comes alive through animation that illustrates what is happening to them from the inside.[22]

---

[20] Active Cues, "Care Innovation for People with Dementia," n.d., https://tovertafel.com/.

[21] Details on the Kitten Scanner are available via Brown, S. (2017) Simon Leo Brown, "Kitten Scanner: The Fun-Sized MRI Machine Changing Lives at Monash Children's Hospital – ABC News (Australian Broadcasting Corporation)," ABC News, 2017.

[22] Roberto Verganti, "Designing Breakthrough Products: How Companies Can Systematically Create Innovations That Customers Don't Even Want," *Harvard Business Review* 89, no. 10 (2011): 114–20.

Fig. 7.7 Kitten Scanner

The Kitten Scanner creates a positive and interactive experience for the child in the waiting room and in preparation for the scan through story-telling, imaging and real-time feedback. This safe and encouraging environment helps the child to understand how the CT scanner works, creating a positive experience association and breaking down the fear that often occurs when children are introduced to the real machine without any kind of preparation.

SnowWorld: Distraction with Virtual Reality

Healing from a burn is often as painful as the experience of the burn itself. Wound care requires the removal of staples and stitches and cleaning dead skin from the wound. Painkillers are often given to patients to help them overcome the excruciating pain, however, in some cases the use of drugs can have carry-on effects.

SnowWorld is a virtual reality game that can distract patients with a realistic snow-filled virtual world with ice and penguins. It has been carefully developed to target patients physiologically to allow them to be fully immersed in the three-dimensional computer-generated world. In SnowWorld patients are empowered to throw snowballs at snowmen, penguins and flying fish with slight movements of their head. The creator of SnowWorld explains that was designed to provide a contrasting scenario to that of fire and heat.[23]

Patients who undergo wound care have reported that their pain levels drop dramatically while playing SnowWorld. The researchers understood the game had to be distracting yet simple enough to play for a patient who is heavily medicated and in pain. This design has been a game changer for burn victims, simply by understanding the issue from all perspectives and capitalising on modern-day technology and psychological distraction. As an entire product, SnowWorld relies on graphic design and experience design.

Incubators: One Size Does Not Fit All

The story of the incubator begins in the late 1870s, when obstetrician Stephane Tarnier went to the Paris zoo and saw an exhibition of chicken incubators.[24] The first human incubator was a hot water bottle stored below a wooden box that housed the baby. This warm enclosure was continually improved and eventually led to the device we know today. However, the incubator can still be improved.

Firefly is an incubator designed by Design that Matters for low-resource hospitals with inexperienced staff.[25] It addresses three key issues. First, medical staff were placing more than one baby into incubators, which pushed them out of the effective area of light. The solution was to

---

[23] As seen on the official website of the Human Photonics Laboratory, "Virtual Reality Pain Reduction," n.d., https://depts.washington.edu/.

[24] Background information on incubators can be found at Columbia University Irving Medical Center, "History of Medicine: The Incubator Babies of Coney Island," n.d., https://columbiasurgery.org/.

[25] Additional information on the firefly incubator can be found at https://www.designthatmatters.org/.

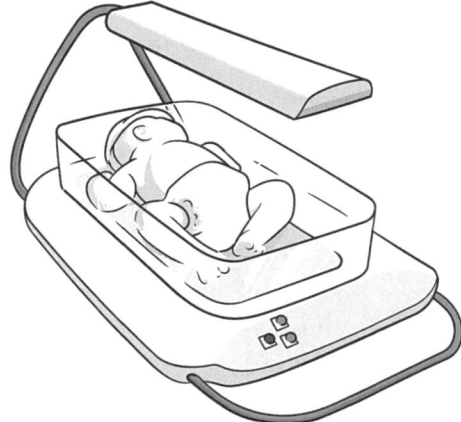

Fig. 7.8   Firefly incubator

design an incubator that could only hold one baby at a time. Second, staff lacked confidence with the treatment even after training, and would cover babies with blankets as they thought the baby was cold. This practice prevented the life-saving light from reaching the babies' skin. The third issue was the separation between mother and newborn, resulting in a reduction in breastfeeding and bonding time. The solution was to create smaller, portable devices that could be placed in the same bed as the mother. Firefly (see Fig. 7.8) was designed to be hard to use incorrectly, simple to clean, effective, energy efficient, easily manoeuvred and functional for five years of 24/7 use.

NeoNurture,[26] also designed by Design that Matters, was created for millions of at-risk infants in developing nations. The rationale for the product is that most incubators are too expensive for many poorer nations. Donated incubators were either not understood, or found to break within five years due to limited or non-existent support for maintenance or repair. NeoNurture was designed to take advantage of local car parts in these regions, such as using headlights for heating elements and dashboard fans for heat/air circulation.

---

[26] Details on NeoNurture incubator can be found at https://www.designthatmatters.org/.

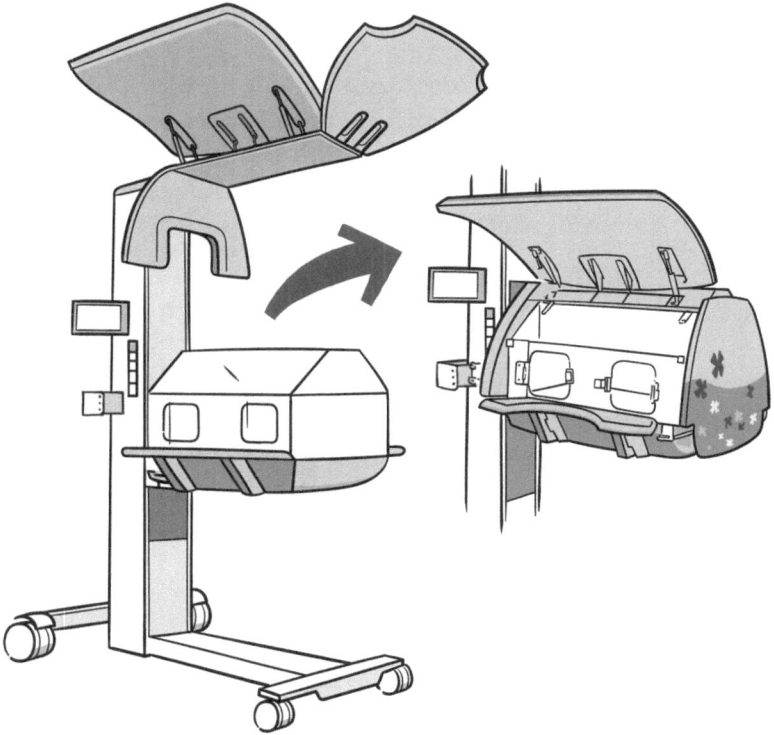

Fig. 7.9 BabyBloom incubator open (left) and closed (right)

Finally, the BabyBloom[27] incubator was designed for removing or reducing parents' fear of the 'technological' or 'clinical' environment of an incubator ward (see Fig. 7.9). The design aims to provide a sense of protection and safety. BabyBloom does this with a shield that covers the incubator, reducing noise and light, which can affect a newborn's health. The incubator is height adjustable, allowing it to be placed over the mother's bed or next to a wheelchair, enabling contact time within the

---

[27] Information about BabyBloom is at Graham Smith, "The Hi-Tech Incubator That Allows a Mother to Bond with Sick Baby from Her Bed… and It Even Comes with an in-Built Video Camera," Daily Mail, 2012, https://www.dailymail.co.uk/.

first hours of a baby's life. The overall design of BabyBloom was fashioned to create a home nursery-like environment.

These three incubators incorporate unique design considerations that serve not only to protect premature or sick infants, but also to address the needs of parents and caregivers. The three incubators illustrate the range of constrains and considerations surrounding a product when designed for different stakeholders or in different sociocultural contexts.

Empowerment Through Experiential Design

Empowering patients through experiential design is vital in the context of health and medicine as it ensures patients interact with the environment around them appropriately. While it can often be a secondary concern for a designer, or even an afterthought, the experiential parameters of the designs described in the case studies have played a pivotal role in encouraging such behaviours.

Summarising Design for Empowerment

Design for empowerment features an external frame of view and is concerned with the wellbeing of healthcare patients and all recipients of care. Three typologies were discussed in design for empowerment: promoting ability, confidence instillers and experiential design. Through these typologies we explored how the four orders of design are used to empower individuals by:

- assisting in minimising and, in some cases, negating medical challenges
- assisting patients in developing confidence and the ability to retain control over their own life
- providing patients with well-designed experiences that often have other significant outcomes for stakeholders.

The impacts and implications of design for empowerment include:

- illustrating that not all issues require clinical solutions
- involving patients is a requisite of determining a successful solution
- supplementing medical treatments through consideration of the patient experience
- identifying patterns and constructing overviews to gain a better understanding of patient needs.

Design for empowerment is focused on tailoring healthcare to the individual—taking into account the patient's priorities, as well as their physiological and psychosocial factors. Table 7.2 describes the four orders of design across the typologies, providing examples of considerations and constraints to be considered when designing solutions for empowerment.

Summarising Part I

Four outcomes emerging from design in health and medicine were introduced in Part I: design for *capacity, knowledge, enablement* and *empowerment*. These outcomes were supported by case studies, which were further segmented across several typologies. Collectively, these outcomes, typologies and case studies demonstrate the ways in which design has been used in the context of health and medicine. Specifically, these illustrate that design caters for challenges (is reactive) and opportunities (is proactive), and that designs are not only internally facing (i.e., cater to practitioners of care) but also externally facing (i.e., cater to recipients of care). In addition, these case studies illustrate how the various domains of design are used individually and collectively in health and medicine.

It is important to note that the outcomes we introduced are not exhaustive, and that we do not expect a given design to cater exclusively to one outcome. Indeed, practitioners may seek to achieve a number of outcomes through their designs. Nevertheless, we argue that for design to be successful, it is important to first consider its intended outcomes. Selecting an outcome includes asking what the driver for innovation is and who the outcome is intended for.

Table 7.2 Design for empowerment considerations and constraints

Order	Description	Considerations	Constraints
(1) Graphic design	Graphic design for empowerment focuses on effectively communicating information to users regardless of ambient conditions or the user's sensory abilities. It includes exploration of different modes (symbolic, verbal, tactile, colours, static and variable) of communication to engage and empower a variety of different users	• Different modes of communication might be more appropriate for different users (e.g. animations for children) • Use of passive (e.g. contrasting colours for colour-blind) or active (slogan or song to provide instructions, e.g. 'Blue to the sky. Orange to the thigh) cues	• Limited range of channels for communication • Design must often rely on users being able to readily recall information in various context (such as emergencies in remote areas)
(2) Industrial design	Industrial design for empowerment spans beyond function to consider the emotional experience of patients. Such design requires understanding users and the context of use (e.g. a novice may be required to use an EpiPen). Products need to be usable, intuitive and appropriate for a diverse user base. These products should empower individuals to overcome their limitations, and provide the confidence required to live as desired	• Design should be intuitive and not rely on prior training • Minimise hazards and adverse consequences from accidental actions and complexity • Design for misuse: make incorrect use or assembly difficult	• Requirement of approval process, device registration and listing • Notification requirements for any repair, replacement, and refund on products • Should be usable without input from experts or professionals

(3) Interaction design	Interaction design for empowerment is about giving people control over themselves and assisting them to surpass limitations emerging from medical conditions. Such interactions build confidence with how new designs are used, assist individuals with doing things in their own time and way, and allow individuals to forget or overcome their pain or condition	• Empowering people to feel more independent can be a risk if something goes awry • How interactions can best compliment products and systems to create long-lasting change • A good experience is paramount to compliance and acceptance of a design	• Diversity of individuals' needs and requirements • Willingness and capacity of users to engage with a design • Outcome can be limited if used as a standalone design
(4) System design	System design for empowerment describes how our systems can assist in empowering individuals. Such design is often focused on accessibility and equality, ensuring that designs reach and consider the broadest range of stakeholders possible. Examples include reusing old prosthetics in developing countries and ensuring that individuals have access to the medical care or products they require	• Measure what matters—consider patient experience alongside medical outcomes • Design for involvement of variety of stakeholders (direct and indirect) • There are often multiple systems to design within and for • Opportunities can stem from understanding how value flows between system stakeholders	• Existing methods and processes for measuring outcomes • Access to stakeholders in the design process • Focus is often short-term rather than long-term • Restrictions emerging from laws, regulations, and from designing across multiple systems

Beyond an introduction and definition for each of these outcomes, we have also outlined a set of design considerations and constraints that correspond to the outcomes and the four orders of design. As seen through the 27 case studies presented in Part I, the outcomes of design are not limited to one discipline of design and often span a number, if not all, of the disciplines. Table 7.3 provides a summary of the design outcomes, along with their aim, corresponding typologies and case studies, outcomes, impact and implications. Guided by this knowledge, Part II illustrates *how* a design process could be structured to achieve these outcomes.

Table 7.3 Summary of design outcomes

Design outcomes	Aim	Typologies	Case studies	Impact and implications
Design for capacity (internal and opportunity driven)	Improving medical processes and reducing strain on the medical sector	Information systems	• Concrn • HealthMap • Defibrillator drones • Driverless ambulances	• Highlighted the need for efficiency and effectiveness in our products, interactions and systems • Automation of services and more timely responses to health-related events
		System automation		• Reduction of workload and labour • More consistent services
		Efficiency innovations	• Nurse handover • CT scanner	• Reduction of human error in healthcare • Improved capacity to deliver timely and informed healthcare services
Design for knowledge (external and opportunity driven)	Informing society to promote preventative healthcare and gather resources for medical research	Blueprints	• Thrive Project • Hospitable hospice	• Assist in the dissemination of knowledge • More considered and accessible templates for design
		Awareness	• Ice Bucket Challenge • World's Greatest Shave	• Raise awareness and funds to tackle prominent healthcare challenges • Provide relevant and contextual healthcare information to the general public
		Visual communication	• Packaging pills • Rescue Rashie	• Reduce strain on healthcare systems through a focus on prevention

(continued)

Table 7.3 (continued)

Design outcomes	Aim	Typologies	Case studies	Impact and implications
Design for enablement (internal and problem driven)	Assist practitioners to perform medical procedures and services to the best of their ability	Procedural instruments Diagnostics	• Trocar • 3D printing • Pap smear speculum • Wong-Baker Pain Scale • Stethoscope • Ultrasound machine	• Provision of the tools and training required to perform medical procedures • Development of methods to capture data that informs decision making • Optimisation of procedures and processes • Customised solutions and assistive tools to reduce surgery time and patient trauma • New platforms and methods for medical education and training
Design for empowerment (external and problem driven)	Improve quality of life and assist individuals with disabilities or acute conditions to face adversity	Promoting ability Confidence instillers Experiential design	• Liftware • Cochlear • TickleFLEX • EpiPen • Tango Belt • Tovertafel Original • Kitten Scanner • SnowWorld • Incubator	• Assist in minimising and, in some cases, negating medical challenges • Assist patients in developing confidence and the ability to retain control over their own life • Healthcare is not just about quantity of life, but also quality of life • Patient experience is an optimal part of healthcare and not all issues require clinical solutions • Involving patients in design is a requisite of determining a successful solution • Patients can serve a significant role in their own healthcare

Part II

Design

In the writing of this book we have observed the expanded role that design plays in society. Indeed, as the discipline of design continues to grow and receive increasing attention, and as the role of design continues to expand, there is a need to better understand the future opportunities that will emerge.

Part I of this book detailed the types of contributions emerging from the discipline of design in the context of health and medicine. These contributions have been categorised according to the four major outcomes we have observed to emerge from such design: *capacity*, *knowledge*, *enablement* and *empowerment*. With these outcomes and disciplines in mind, Part II illustrates *how* a design process should be structured in order to maximise outcomes in this unique context.

Part II is split across three major sections. In Chap. 8 we describe the components of our medical design innovation framework, an iterative process that assists in translating a design concept or idea into tangible outcomes. Chapter 9 is comprised of three primary case studies that illustrate the framework. The first case study describes an organisation seeking to reimagine the ageing experience through an innovative business model offering. The second case study details the process of start-up company Glucotek Inc. and the development of a solution for supporting women with Gestational Diabetes Mellitus (GDM). The third case study describes a number of design initiatives to support ventricular assist device (VAD) stakeholders. Finally, in Chap. 10 we present a set of design principles and actions to assist in transitioning design from a concept to practice. The book concludes with our final thoughts.

8

The Process

The medical sector has a unique set of challenges and constraints for which design innovation is well suited. Design innovation requires looking beyond what is known in order to identify the root issue, which may not be immediately evident. When faced with a problem, it is human nature to jump to a solution using habitual thinking patterns. Overcoming this tendency in favour of 'thinking outside the box' allows us to question the problem to understand if it is indeed the right problem to be addressing. By reframing the 'wrong' question we can get the 'right' answer. Jumping to a solution without fully understanding the problem destroys the potential value that a solution may offer.[1] More is to be gained by taking the time to question what the real problem is and by uncovering the needs of those involved.

There is evidence to suggest the increasing prominence of design in health and medicine—both within design practice and academia. Yet little has been published to assist individuals seeking to implement design innovation.[2] This is a particular challenge in health and medicine, given

---

[1] Cara Wrigley, "Principles and Practices of a Design-Led Approach to Innovation," *International Journal of Design Creativity and Innovation* 5, no. 3–4 (2017): 235–55.

[2] Wrigley, 2016.

© The Author(s) 2020
E. Nusem et al., *Design Innovation for Health and Medicine*,
https://doi.org/10.1007/978-981-15-4362-3_8

the need for regulation and multiple stage gates of approval for medical design.

In this chapter we therefore demonstrate the design process, and focus on the context of design, the intended outcomes of design, and the types of design that might be used in a given project. As previously discussed, the design process can be broadly captured in four distinct phases: insight, intent, design and action. In this portion of the book we elaborate on the model further—introducing *consider* and *audit* as components that form insight, and *implement* and *evaluate* as components that form action. This relationship is illustrated in Fig. 8.1.

Insight is generally formed by an understanding of two aspects. First, *consider*, in which an understanding of the design's legacy and 'context' (where the design takes place) are developed. This includes developing an understanding of both the external factors in the environment (such as regulatory constraints) and internal factors (such as appetite for innovation and system requirements that might exist within an organisation). The second aspect is *audit*, in which an analysis is conducted to provide insight into a combination of market trends, latent user needs and/or existing offerings. Together, consider and audit form the insight(s) that can later be framed into intent. Collectively, these two modes are structured to capture *why* a design should take place, along with *what* opportunities or challenges the design might address.

Intent, as discussed in Part I of the book, entails the framing of desired outcomes based on known insights. Once intent and the associated

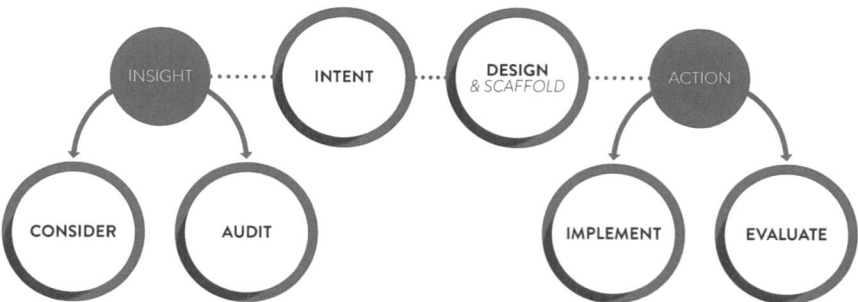

Fig. 8.1 Medical design innovation process

outcomes have been determined, one can begin to design and scaffold with consideration of all orders (disciplines) of design. When referring to scaffolding, we describe the process of using additional modes of design to support a core design component. Examples of this include: the EpiPen (see p. 81), where graphic design (first order of design) was used to support industrial design (second order of design) through the instructions that indicate how the device should be used; or HealthMap (see p. 27), an electronic information system that uses informal online sources for disease outbreaks (fourth order of design), and makes them accessible through a number of mobile applications (third order of design). Without these additional components (or 'scaffolding', as we refer to it in this text), it would be difficult for these designs to function as intended.

The design process has been covered extensively in the literature, with many design methodologies being established and widely used in academia and practice. Consequently, this book does not offer a design methodology, but rather speaks to the dimensions that are needed to support design so that new outputs are able to flourish in healthcare. In addition, we elaborate on the individual and collective role of the design disciplines, with a focus on their interrelationships. Many design frameworks overlook action: the implementation and evaluation of outputs. Implementation, however, serves as an important aspect of design. Without implementation, outputs would remain as concepts that offer little in developing the field and practice. Evaluation is also integral: assessing whether the designed outputs perform as anticipated and whether the intended outcomes of the design have been met. A summary of these six stages is provided in Table 8.1. The framework builds upon Kolb,[3] Owen,[4] and Beckman and Barry's[5] models, and applies design concepts such as a user needs approach (empathy) not only to the end-user (or customer), but also to stakeholders.

Like many design processes and methods, the framework depicted here is iterative, with success measured through the fulfilment of the

---

[3] David A. Kolb, *Experience as the Source of Learning and Development* (Upper Sadle River: Prentice Hall, 1984).

[4] Charles L. Owen, "Design Research: Building the Base," *Design Studies* 19, no. 1 (1998): 9–20.

[5] Sara L. Beckman and Michael Barry, "Innovation as a Learning Process: Embedding Design Thinking," *California Management Review* 50, no. 1 (2007): 25–56.

Table 8.1   Overview of medical design innovation stages

Design stage	Purpose
Consider	Understanding the context in which design is to take place, the legacy of any designs being superseded and the conditions for design. Factors influencing these include appetite for the design (both internally within any affiliated organisations and externally within the broader industry) and the presence of any systems to support or hinder the design
Audit	An investigation of market conditions, the current state of a product or service, stakeholders' latent needs, and/or the opportunities that exist within a given context. Audits are structured to identify the insight(s) that frame intent, and to inform the intended outcomes of design
Intent	Establishing what the outcomes of the design should be (e.g. *capacity, knowledge, enablement* or *empowerment*). Intent is integral in the translation of design, requiring an accurate definition of the challenge or opportunity addressed and an understanding of how success can be measured. This is not about determining what the design should be
Design/ scaffold	The practices utilised to conceptualise and develop the design, and to determine which additional modes of design can be utilised to best support a core design component
Implement	The path of implementation selected to translate design into practice (i.e. taking a design from a concept or idea into a tangible reality). Factors include a market entry strategy, a plan for growth and scaling, and developing an ecosystem in which the design can thrive
Evaluate	Determining quantitative and qualitative metrics for assessing whether the design can be considered a success, and establishing whether the design has met its intended outcomes as determined earlier in the design innovation process

intended outcome. The 'medical design innovation framework' is illustrated in Fig. 8.2. It is important to note that while a recommended order is illustrated in the process, this order is not absolute. The framework has been designed to illustrate the ideal order when working with a 'blank canvas'; however, design rarely occurs in a vacuum. Indeed, design is rarely so simple, and good design is influenced by an understanding of the present circumstances and any past activity that might be relevant. For example, when engaged by an organisation to help redesign one of their products or services, a practitioner might opt to follow the mode of

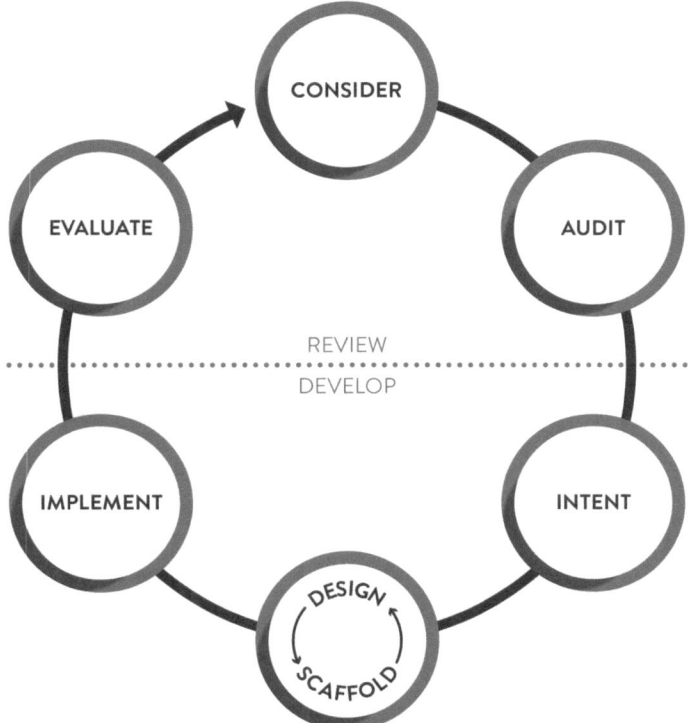

Fig. 8.2   Medical design innovation framework

'consider' with 'evaluate' in order to better understand the shortcomings of an existing design. The practitioner might then proceed in an order different to that outlined in the model, given what they find while evaluating the previous design. The following sections detail each of the phases in the framework in more detail.

Stage A: Consider

Consider refers to the context in which design occurs and the legacy of previous or existing designs. Considering these two components is a prerequisite of successful design and can help to determine the future direction and scope of work. These two components may differ significantly based on factors including context, maturity of the market or concept, and/or societal understandings or expectations of the design. Understanding the history of the design does not usually require a formal process of investigation. Most design in health and medicine occurs (or at least should occur) with the involvement of subject matter experts, or even be directed and practised by a subject matter expert. In the former scenario, the expert can brief the designer about the current state of the design and its context.

When speaking of context we largely refer to the conditions in which the design exists—both internally (e.g. the organisation seeking to design) and externally (e.g. the industry sector in which design is taking place)—which can inform whether design can or should occur. Indeed, lacking an understanding of conditions results in many designs not receiving the support required or overlooking regulatory constraints. Such designs are often met with failure or prevented from functioning as intended (or at all). An example of this was presented in Part I, where a case on defibrillator drones was discussed (see p. 29). Implementation of the drones proved to be a major issue due to existing flightpath regulations. Considering the context of use and major stakeholders for the drones during initial stages of development could have potentially helped to highlight and address this issue. These setbacks often occur when design is executed in a silo, with little attention being paid to the surrounding environment.

A number of texts describe the ideal conditions for design,[6] whether in organisations or larger government bodies. While much of this can be translated into the context of health and medicine, the health sector also has a host of other organisations, such as non-profits and charities, that operate in their own unique manner.

Ensuring that the right conditions are present, or establishing these conditions, is integral and the first step of the process outlined in this

---

[6] Ulla-Maaria Mutanen, "Developing Organisational Design Capability in a Finland-Based Engineering Corporation: The Case of Metso," *Design Studies* 29, no. 5 (2008): 500–520; Erez Nusem, Cara Wrigley, and Judy Matthews, "Developing Design Capability in Nonprofit Organizations," *Design Issues* 33, no. 1 (2017): 61–75.

chapter.[7] Design, lacking internal support through the right conditions, is unlikely to result in long-term success within an organisation. Beyond these internal conditions, it is also important to be conscious of the external conditions in which one is designing. External conditions vary based on the medical stream being explored, but are generally composed of regulatory constraints, system requirements, emerging market trends and ethics. Essentially, these external conditions form stage gates for translation of medical design. Understanding external conditions requires expertise in the field or an audit—as discussed in the following section.

Stage B: Audit

Audits are conducted to develop an understanding of market and user needs with the aim of informing intent. A plethora of methods exist to help with conducting an audit to identify market trends and latent user needs. However, depending on existing knowledge and expertise in the design context, any combination of these two dimensions may be recommended. For example, design stemming from an opportunity implies some form of insight, such as an unmet user need. Here, the recommended approach could be to investigate the functions of a range of designs and compare these functions to users' needs.[8] This process could serve to identify user needs that are not met by existing designs, thus framing the intent of design. Likewise, identifying a gap in competitors' business model typologies might serve to inform insight, and help to inform the intent of the design by framing the latent user needs that could be addressed through the identified gap.[9]

Indeed, audits can assist in developing an understanding of market conditions, the current state of a product or service, highlight

---

[7] Cara Wrigley, Erez Nusem, and Karla Straker, "Implementing Design Thinking: Understanding Organizational Conditions," *California Management Review*, 2020.

[8] For an example of this process see Keum Hee Kimmi Ko et al., "A Comparative Content Analysis of Digital Channels for Ventricular Assist Device Patients, Caregivers, and Healthcare Practitioners," *American Society of Artificial Internal Organs* 65, no. 8 (2019): 855–63.

[9] For an example of this process, see Nusem, E., Wrigley, C. and Matthews, J. (2017b) 'Exploring aged care business models : A typological study', *Ageing and Society*, 37(2), pp. 386–409.

stakeholders' latent needs, and/or the opportunities that exist within a given context. An audit can be constructed through the analysis of secondary data (following a methodology such as content analysis), and can help the designer develop some expertise in the field before engaging with real people (which can be time consuming and costly). In healthcare, this stage can also serve to inform the designer of external conditions and to establish whether the design is feasible. If the design doesn't already exist (in some form), this may be for good reason—regulations may be too prohibitive, the technology may be too experimental or the design may not clearly address a stakeholder need.

Qualitative approaches (e.g. semi-structured interviews or focus groups) relying on the collection of primary data are also an excellent method for conducting an audit. As well as acting as a stand-alone audit, these methods can be used to support and confirm findings from a preliminary analysis of secondary data. This step ensures that the preliminary findings are valid, and establishes trust in the direction chosen by the designer. Qualitative approaches with primary data can be more complex, as they require a prior understanding of the design context, ethical considerations (depending on the institute from which design is stemming) and are noticeable (unlike a content analysis, which can be conducted discreetly).

Regardless of the approach selected, the primary function of an audit is to discover insight(s) that can be used to frame the intent of design and establish outcomes the design aims to achieve. We encourage intent to be informed by an understanding of both market direction/trends and latent user needs.

Stage C: Intent

Once an understanding of the design context and challenges or opportunities have been established the designer can begin to scope out their intent. This stage is not about determining what the design itself should be, but rather establishing what the outcomes of design should be. We've identified four outcomes of design in the context of health and medicine (as detailed in Part I), and these can be used to assist design practitioners to establish what they intend their respective design(s) to accomplish, prior to designing. As illustrated in Part I, design outcomes in health and medicine span across two dimensions. First, whether they are opportunity or problem driven (proactive or reactive), and second, whether they are internal or external (for practitioners or recipients). The outcomes themselves—capacity, knowledge, enablement and empowerment—assist in framing the intent of design. We do not consider these outcomes to be exhaustive, nor do we expect a design to sit exclusively within one of these categories (as some practitioners may seek to achieve a number of outcomes through their designs). However, having a clear intent and purpose is critical for the successful translation of design outcomes, and is dependent on having an accurate definition of the problem and understanding the metrics of success.

Stage D: Design/Scaffold

There are innumerable design processes and frameworks, each with its own strengths and weaknesses. However, these processes and frameworks are generally comprised of similar structures. The frameworks involve:

- an understanding of stakeholders
- a definition of the problem at hand (whether a challenge or opportunity)
- the conceptualisation of solutions
- prototyping of solutions
- testing whether the solutions work (see Fig. 1.3, p. 4).

The intent of this book isn't to offer instructions for designing, but rather to help build an understanding of the broader environment in which design happens. With such an understanding the design can become better informed, and designers can be conscious of the goals to be achieved.

Supporting this intent and realising goals requires that design is holistic and scaffolded (i.e. that the design leverages any number of the four orders of design to support its offering). In practice, many organisations believe that an app (or some other popular, topical design) is the answer to all their struggles. Unfortunately, this is not the case, and each challenge and opportunity presents a unique case to be considered. As described in Maslow's famous quote 'if all you have is a hammer, everything looks like a nail', just because mobile applications are a familiar tool does not necessarily mean they are the best or most appropriate solution for a given problem.

Any order or discipline of design might be relevant, and often a combination of disciplines is the best way of achieving the desired intent. For example, a product might require the support of a business model (system design), a service offering that attracts and retains customers (interaction design), or graphic components that communicate the function of the design or raise awareness of the design itself (graphic design). Indeed, designs shouldn't exist in isolation, and it's important to consider how each design should be scaffolded. This shouldn't be done for the sake of it, and not all designs require all orders. The orders should be strategically selected to help a design thrive and meet its intent.

Stage E: Implement

Implementation is about bringing the design into the real world and is perhaps the most difficult component of medical design. Coming up with an idea (good or bad) is relatively simple. Turning that idea into reality is a whole other matter. Unfortunately, there is no one method or 'cookie-cutter' approach for design implementation. Each design and its context are unique, and should be approached as such.

There is no argument that medical designers excel at implementation, bridging the gap between concept and product in a multitude of instances, in perhaps one of the most challenging disciplines. However, this implementation often focuses more on the technical considerations of a design, rather than meeting patient needs. Implementation is also composed of a number of other factors, including market entry strategy, a plan for growth and scaling, and an ecosystem in which the design can thrive. Likewise, many design processes don't take these factors into account, and conclude once testing has been conducted.

There are a number of paths to implementing design outputs in health-care, necessitating not only commercial considerations, but also bureau-cratic and regulatory ones. Medical devices, for example, require submission of Premarket Approval or Premarket Notification to regula-tory bodies such as the U.S. Food and Drug Administration (FDA). The uncertainty of approval and an unknown launch date make for a chal-lenge in determining a path to implementation and establishing revenue. In addition, there is a need to balance social and economic impact. For example, a design that focuses on social impact can bypass a number of implementation challenges by being open-sourced (following design and testing), providing access to those who need it most (like case studies explored in the blueprint typology in Part I, p. 43). However, such designs don't directly generate revenue. It's vital to select an appropriate path to implementation.

Stage F: Evaluate

The final stage is evaluation. Here, it is determined whether the intent and associated outcome(s) have been achieved. Evaluation requires an understanding of the metrics of success: the measurements assessed to establish whether the design has accomplished what was intended. These metrics are often quantitative and clinical in nature, but it is important to also consider more qualitative metrics such as quality of life. Markets can move quickly, and at times a pivot or amendment to the design might be required to achieve the intended outcomes.

Even once an intended outcome has been achieved, this may not be the case forever. We live in a rapidly developing society and it is impor-tant to remain vigilant for new opportunities or emerging challenges. Design is, after all, an iterative process. It is our hope that through this framework designers will be better able to translate their concepts into tangible outputs for health and medicine.

9

Utilising Design

Through this book we have made two main theoretical contributions. First, we have identified four outcomes that emerge from design in health and medicine and framed these outcomes as *intent*. Second, we have introduced the medical design innovation framework (see Fig. 8.2) to assist anyone seeking to design in the context of health and medicine. In this chapter we further detail the framework through three primary case studies. These case studies outline how the framework can be applied in different contexts, along with how the modes within the framework can be reordered to adapt to a given context.

This chapter is therefore comprised of three case studies that outline the role of the framework. The first case details an aged care organisation seeking to redefine the experience of ageing through an offering focusing on early engagement and prevention. This case depicts how the framework can be applied when design is used within an organisation that is aware of the deficits of its existing offering, and has interest in designing new and innovative alternatives. The second case study describes the development of a digital channel to support women with Gestational Diabetes Mellitus. The digital channel was designed as an early market entry strategy for a wearable technology that was being developed. The

© The Author(s) 2020
E. Nusem et al., *Design Innovation for Health and Medicine*,
https://doi.org/10.1007/978-981-15-4362-3_9

third case outlines a number of design initiatives to support and scaffold a ventricular assist device—a device to support patients suffering from advanced heart failure.[1] These cases are presented through the medical design innovation framework outlined in Chap. 8.

Bravo: Redefining the Ageing Experience

In this section we present a case study on an organisation seeking to redefine the ageing experience through a new start-up (Bravo).[2] The case study organisation—RSL Care, a non-profit aged care provider—sought to differentiate from the homogeneous offering in the market, and to empower the elderly by guiding positive behavioural change through a business model that offers advice, motivation and connection. Data were collected over a 24-month action research study, where the researcher was embedded within the organisation. The organisation's design journey followed the process detailed in Chap. 8: consider, audit, intent, design/scaffold, implement and evaluate.

Consider

The external conditions for change were ideal, with aged care providers being challenged to respond to an increasingly discerning customer base, major changes to regulation and an ageing population. As a result, many providers began to question the value of their services, and the ways in which these services were delivered. Beyond the negative stigma of aged care services, disruptions in the market compelled organisations to investigate alternative models of aged care. However, given the highly regulated nature of aged care, there were significant constraints, largely related to funding, on how innovation could occur.

---

[1] Robert V. Snyders, Ventricular assist device, 4,690,134 (Washington, DC: U.S. Patent and Trademark Office, issued 1987).

[2] This case study elaborates on work that was initially published as a book chapter in International Perspectives on Business Innovation and Disruption in Design. For more information see Erez Nusem, Cara Wrigley, and Judy Matthews, "Disrupting the Aged Care Business Model," in *International Perspectives on Business Innovation and Disruption in Design*, ed. Robert DeFillippi, Alison Rieple, and Patrik Wikstorm (Edward Elgar Publishing, 2016), 17–35.

From an internal perspective, the organisation knew it needed to undergo significant change—yet it had a limited understanding of design's potential contributions (beyond those generally associated with the built environment, such as architecture). As such, the organisation's understanding of design had to be developed alongside the development of design outputs. This took place across four stages: demonstrating the value of design, conceptualising design outputs, implementing the design outputs, and integrating design within the organisation.

Audit

Initial stages of research saw RSL Care set out to better understand its customer demographic and competitive environment. They conducted an audit consisting of an in-depth customer segmentation study and a content analysis of their competitors. Insights uncovered through the audit informed not only what the organisation would design, but also *why* it would design (i.e., its intent).

The customer segmentation study was comprised of qualitative and quantitative components relating to the needs, preferences, attitudes, behaviours and decision-making approaches of ageing Australians and their families. Over 90 hours of qualitative data (consisting of in-depth and paired in-depth interviews and focus groups) were collected in metropolitan and regional areas across the eastern seaboard of Australia.[3] Findings from the qualitative research informed the design of a quantitative data collection approach, incorporating over 1300 surveys deployed through telephone and online methods. The research revealed that older Australians wanted the experience of ageing and aged care to shift from a disease focus (reactive) to a holistic wellbeing focus (proactive), and the development of services that motivate positive ageing behaviours that extend healthy life expectancy.[4] In addition, the research approach resulted in a rich bank of qualitative and quantitative insights concerning the experience of ageing, and a segmentation model describing five unique customer segments and four unique

---

[3] Nusem, Wrigley, and Matthews.
[4] As articulated by the organisation's Chief Customer Officer in "'Bravo' to RSL Care!", *Aged Care Guide* (2015), https://www.agedcareguide.com.au/.

'influencer' segments.[5] These findings heavily influenced and grounded the direction of the project. Principally, the research revealed two major clusters in the five customer segments: (i) the organisation's existing customer base, with low levels of financial comfort and an external locus of control; and (ii) the organisation's desired customers, with high levels of financial comfort and an internal locus of control.

The content analysis component saw the researchers analyse the business models—an organisation's operational plan, consisting of the value delivered to an organisation's customers, as well as how this value is delivered—of 37 Australian aged care providers.[6] The 'business model canvas'[7] was used to investigate the common business model typologies used by aged care providers; the viability of existing aged care business model typologies; and the capacity of existing models of care in meeting the emerging needs of an ageing population. The analysis highlighted a number of challenges testing the aged care sector's capacity to adapt and meet emerging customer needs and supply issues. Additionally, the audit allowed the organisation to better understand its competitors, and identified six overarching aged care business model typologies.[8]

Intent

RSL Care knew it needed to shift from its homogeneous business model in order to adapt to changing regulatory conditions, an ageing population and customers with increasing demands. But it didn't jump straight into *what* it should be designing, but rather asked *why* it should be designing. The organisation was able to frame its intent by building on insights gathered through the audit: to redefine the ageing experience, with the goal of empowering the elderly.

---

[5] Nusem, Wrigley, and Matthews, "Disrupting the Aged Care Business Model."

[6] Erez Nusem, Cara Wrigley, and Judy Matthews, "Exploring Aged Care Business Models : A Typological Study," *Ageing and Society* 37, no. 2 (2017): 386–409.

[7] Alexander Osterwalder and Yves Pigneur, *Business Model Generation: A Handbook for Visionaries, Game Changers, and Challengers* (Wiley, 2010).

[8] For more information about the content analysis and findings see Nusem, Wrigley, and Matthews, "Exploring Aged Care Business Models : A Typological Study."

Design/Scaffold

RSL Care designed a new business model that would promote healthy ageing for customers, reducing the risk of chronic disease and preventable conditions, and empowering customers to enjoy a healthier, more productive and purposeful second half of life. The design process took place across three phases. The first phase saw the organisation test its assumptions and findings from the audit. The second phase saw the organisation conceptualise ideas to address its customers' issues and needs, and to better align to future market needs. The third phase saw the organisation prototype, test and scaffold its ideas and finally launch a new start-up organisation.

In the first phase of design the organisation conducted a set of narrative focus groups, with an emphasis on co-designing with customers. The narrative was used to test customer insights, and conceptualise how these insights could be leveraged into new business models by iteratively challenging the organisation's assumptions. With confirmation of why they needed to design, the organisation sought to ideate and develop initial solutions. During this phase the organisation designed and conducted three focus groups with separate foci:

1. Customer journey mapping,[9] with the aim of identifying the needs of stakeholders and 'white space' for new business model opportunities in the aged care sector.
2. Customer immersion and ideation, with the aim of exploring a number of dimensions across the ageing experience (e.g. 'Staying Connected').
3. Customer co-design, with the aim of co-designing outputs with participants and synthesising a new business model.

The business model centred around an offering to maximise individuals' working and healthy life expectancy, empowering the elderly to have a purpose and providing a means for the elderly to be productive

---

[9] A journey map is a visual interpretation of a customer's interaction with a business, often used by designers to detail the process of a person seeking to accomplish a goal.

members of society. As a system, the business model was scaffolded through a number of other design outputs as shown in Table 9.1.

It is no great surprise that traditional aged care services are somewhat stigmatised. Bravo, based on the new business model, was designed as a start-up to compete with traditional aged care services through a proactive approach focusing on prevention. The start-up aimed to meet more than just the customers' basic needs (physical and mental health), but also their higher-order needs (such as having a purpose and being a productive member of society). Bravo's business model (see Fig. 9.1) sought to provide trusted advice, motivation and connection for customers earlier in life—accomplished through the provision of health and medicine programs that extend healthy life expectancy, and new forms of living for the second half of life, with a focus on restorative environments connected to local communities.[10]

Several design outputs supported the business model, including an application, services and targeted branding. Bravo's service was designed to assist people to prolong their healthy life expectancy. Customers would come in and be connected to a personal wellness guide, who would conduct an initial consultation. The customer would then set up a range of goals, with the aim of creating a healthy and sustainable lifestyle. This ensured that customers would be as prepared as possible for retirement

Table 9.1 RSL Care design outputs

Order	Description
1. Graphic design	Vibrant and casual logo design to engage the target demographic of users
2. Industrial design	Design of an app to connect customers to a team of expert channels (providing advice, motivation and connection), allowing customers to set goals and measure their progress
3. Interaction design	Wellness Guide (a personal coach and advisor) to help facilitate their induction into the new service offering and assist to set up their goals and connect them to partner suppliers
4. Systems design	Launch of a start-up business model to guide people through their second half of life, with the aim of changing behaviours, reducing the risk of chronic diseases and extending peoples' healthy and working life expectancies

---

[10] For more details on Bravo's offering see the Good Design Australia application "Redefining the Ageing Experience" (2015), https://good-design.org/.

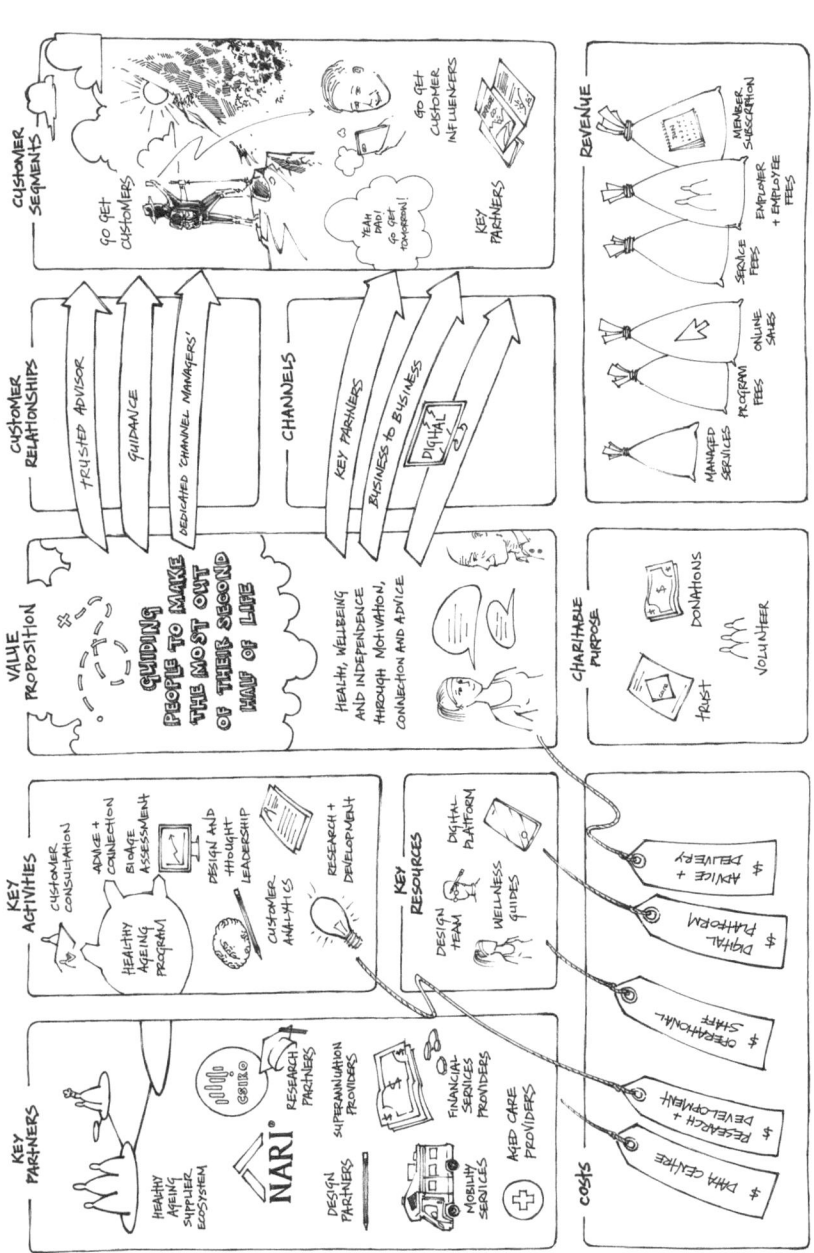

Fig. 9.1 Bravo's business model (Erez Nusem, Cara Wrigley, and Judy Matthews, "Disrupting the Aged Care Business Model," in *International Perspectives on Business Innovation and Disruption in Design*, ed. Robert DeFillippi, Alison Rieple, and Patrik Wikstorm (Edward Elgar Publishing, 2016), 17–35)

and their end of life. Progress was measured through an application that assisted customers to stay motivated and connected, and to get personalised and on-demand advice from experts. The application allowed the user to track their progress (through measurements of bio age and healthy ageing), and connected customers to a range of partner services that offered support and promoted health and wellbeing to like-minded people. Finally, a name and logo were designed to resonate with the business model's target demographic, as illustrated in Fig. 9.2. Bravo's intended impact was 'positive behavioural change that reduces the risk of chronic disease and extends healthy and working life expectancy'.[11]

The prototype was refined and developed, and included an online portal, engagement plan, supplier partnering and staffing structure. Seven focus group sessions with 40 participants from the organisation's desired customer segment were then conducted to ensure the prototype accurately reflected initial insights captured with customers. The focus groups aimed to detail the conceptual model in accordance to customer preferences, and to create a 'minimum viable product'[12] for launch.

Implement

Following the design and scaffolding component, RSL Care designed a strategy for implementing Bravo. Geo-mapping was used to identify areas with high population density and large concentrations of elderly

Fig. 9.2   Bravo branding

---

[11] As articulated by RSL Care in its submission "Redefining the Ageing Experience" to the Good Design Awards, available at https://good-design.org/https://good-design.org/"/.

[12] A minimum viable product is a functional design with minimal features, satisfying initial customers and gathering feedback for further development.

individuals (potential customers), and to select the initial launch site for the prototype. Subsequently, a market analysis of potential suppliers (partners) was conducted. The design team was embedded in the proto-type location, allowing for immersion in the community, and providing insight into the lifestyle and motivations of potential customers.

An online quantitative survey was administered to over 800 partici-pants, with these being recruited based on the segmentation study.[13] The survey captured participants' perceptions of the initial offering and brand, with the aim of understanding: healthy ageing behaviours; propensity to pay for the service; optimal method(s) and channel(s) for engagement; levels and types of chronic disease and how they are managed; education and employment status; life transitions and experiences; and location density of the organisation's target customer segment. Subsequently, the prototype was launched with 26 test users and 14 external suppliers across two suburbs with high concentrations of the organisation's target customer segments.

Evaluate

Despite a positive reception, engaging customers for a preventative ser-vice was challenging. Preventative services are also difficult to market, as outcomes and the return-on-investment can feel intangible. The start-up faced a number of difficulties in scaling the services offered and increas-ing their customer base. Additionally, the start-up did not produce sig-nificant revenue in relation to the investments made for development, and was discontinued following a change of leadership in the parent organisation. This is unfortunate, as preventative services that focus on the wellbeing of customers and assist in keeping the elderly productive and engaged can have significant benefits for society. Nevertheless, until the general populace are able to recognise the value of such services their adoption is going be a difficult endeavour. The discontinuation of the service can also be attributed to its scale in relation to the market. Creating such services, which focus on customers' wellbeing, requires the support of an entire industry sector, not just one organisation.

---

[13] Nusem, Wrigley, and Matthews, "Disrupting the Aged Care Business Model."

Summarising Bravo

This case study has demonstrated how the medical design innovation framework was applied in an organisation seeking to design a new and innovative business model. The design output, as a standalone entity, was ultimately unable to meet its intended outcome and redefine the ageing experience. Design at an industry scale is a new phenomenon and can be observed in this case study. Design in the fourth order has traditionally been concerned with 'networks' and disciplines. Beyond systems and environments, some change is impractical, if not impossible, to realise as a singular entity. Consequently, the focus of design for sectors is on creating scalable platforms that support groups to realise their ambitions. We anticipate the design (or redesign, in some instances) of sectors to become increasingly evident as society continues to develop and becomes more interconnected.

Doula: Supporting Women with Gestational Diabetes Mellitus

This case study describes the winning concept of the Australian MIT Innovation and Entrepreneurship Bootcamp held in 2017. In pursuit of their concept the winning team formed the start-up company known as Glucotek Inc. The team was comprised of four entrepreneurs, including two diabetics, a medical engineer with expertise in blood testing devices, and a computational bio-scientist specialising in diabetes research. Collectively, these individuals were all not only passionate about making blood glucose measurements (which require the patient to prick their finger with a lancet) less invasive, but also about empowering pregnant women to take control of their health during a challenging time. The team designed a wearable device to assist in managing Gestational Diabetes Mellitus (GDM)—a form of diabetes developed by women during pregnancy, characterised by higher than normal blood sugar (glucose) levels.[14] Our team was subsequently engaged to help determine the direction for design while the wearable technology was undergoing the

---

[14]American Diabetes Association, "Gestational Diabetes Mellitus," *Diabetes Care* 27, no. 1 (2004): S88–90.

lengthy FDA approval. The design journey is described through our framework (as seen in Chap. 8), comprising of the phases: consider, audit, intent, design/scaffold and implement.

Consider

A range of external conditions needed consideration when designing methods of managing GDM. From a patient perspective, there was a fairly significant appetite for methods of managing GDM given the risks associated with the disease. Following diagnosis, patients have a short period of time to make significant adjustments to their lifestyles and, although the condition itself is temporary (blood glucose regulates after giving birth), women with GDM are seven times more likely to develop Type 2 diabetes later in life.[15] There was a notable gap in the market for design that assists a woman's journey from diagnosis through to post-birth management with GDM and to adapt to their new (albeit temporary) lifestyle. There was also societal interest, as GDM was the fastest growing type of diabetes in Australia.[16] Unfortunately, the Food and Drug Administration's (FDA) approval process for wearable devices is lengthy, requiring a sound strategy for managing funds, building and maintaining interest and developing the design further.

From an internal conditions perspective, the team developing the design began as a start-up. As such, the organisation was agile but cash poor—relying on external funding to maintain progress. The team had a clear vision for the future, as well as directives, but lacked in people (from a quantitative perspective) and environment (in the sense of a physical presence). Tamara Mills, the inventor and founder, was 30 weeks pregnant at the time of the bootcamp, and had a key insight that informed the concept. Having been diagnosed with GDM, Tamara was aware of the hardships mothers faced following diagnosis, including the invasiveness of blood glucose measurements, the need to learn rapidly during a

[15] Ben Whitelaw and Carol Gayle, "Gestational Diabetes," *Obstetrics, Gynaecology and Reproductive Medicine* 21, no. 2 (2011): 41–46.

[16] Olivia Willis, "Type 2 Diabetes: Understanding Australia's Fastest Growing Chronic Condition," ABC News, 2018, https://www.abc.net.au/.

stressful time, diet and craving control and not knowing what to eat and when.

Tamara's team conceptualised a wearable technology that transmits data on the wearer's blood glucose levels to a patient. Using machine learning, the product (an output of industrial design) is able to predict responses to food prior to consumption. A digital channel (an output of interaction design) would then provide recommendations on what and how much the patient should eat. Since many women have ear piercings, earrings were selected as the wearable technology—providing a non-invasive way for patients to easily monitor and track their glucose levels and present the data appropriately to their medical practitioner. The monitor, encapsulated in a pair of earrings, would remove the need for women to constantly prick their finger to test their glucose levels. The design output would also require a digital communication channel (such as a mobile application) to: convey the clinical importance of measuring and monitoring glucose levels and other related data; visualise the data collected through the wearable technology; present the data in a decipherable way; and inform patients' decision making (in relation to recommended diet and physical activity routines associated with the condition). The goal was to design a wearable technology that would become the industry standard for monitoring blood glucose levels, requiring patient interaction and medical practitioner overview, with these two functions allowing for real time monitoring and feedback.

A large consideration within this project was the long-term goals of medical technology organisation Glucotek Inc. As a start-up in its infancy without other design outputs, the team had to consider how their portfolio could be expanded while awaiting the lengthy FDA approval for the wearable technology. Subsequently, the start-up engaged the University of Sydney to assist in designing the interaction between the product and patient. This involved the development and launch of an application to accompany the device, compatible for use with any blood glucose monitoring device. The application could help establish Glucotek's presence in the market and allow it to acquire a loyal customer base prior to the earrings' release. Following our engagement, the team began with an audit to better understand existing offerings in the market.

Audit

The audit featured two phases. The first phase consisted of a literature review focused on the experiences of women with GDM and existing mobile-based applications, and resulted in the development of the Key Stages of the GDM Patient Journey (see Fig. 9.3).

The second phase involved exploring the current market offering of mobile-based applications on the Apple App and Google Play stores. A total of 46 applications were reviewed and six typologies were identified through the analysis of applications' characteristics.

These typologies illustrate the aspects of management that applications cater for. The analysis also revealed that applications catering for GDM had limited differentiation to those catering for Type 1 and 2 diabetes, and applications often focused on the management and treatment of diabetes (rather than the experience of pregnancy). Notably, applications that validated patients' actions or reduced stress and uncertainty (e.g. medical practitioner overview and real-time feedback, the ability to enter specific data pre- and post-meal, and connecting to other patients with similar circumstances) were well received. No applications were found to span the continuum of the patient journey (as seen in Fig. 9.3). The audit revealed significant gaps in the market, highlighting the opportunity for the development of an application that catered for women during any stage of the GDM patient journey.

Intent

The insights obtained from the external conditions and audit informed the intent: to support pregnant women diagnosed with GDM to take

Fig. 9.3 Key Stages of GDM Patient Journey (courtesy of Lindsay Page and Miranda Phillips)

control of their health. Given that intent was framed around the patient, and is reactive through its response to an existing issue, the intended outcome can be defined as empowerment. This was to be achieved through the alleviation of two issues related to GDM. Firstly, by providing an alternative to existing invasive methods of measuring blood glucose. Secondly, by providing a method for managing blood glucose levels to patients with limited expertise.

Design/Scaffold

A co-design approach was employed, involving key stakeholder groups throughout the design process. The result was the application Doula (see Fig. 9.4).[17] In conjunction with the earring design (see Fig. 9.5), Doula shifts the focus from the condition (GDM) to empowering women to make positive choices for their health and the health of their unborn child; the application reinforces this through reminders of why they should manage their condition. The application allows women to take control of their pregnancy and actively manage their health, with the aim of developing sustained healthy habits to reduce the elevated risk of developing Type 2

Fig. 9.4 Doula concept—designed Lindsay Page and Miranda Phillips

---

[17] Doula was designed by Lindsay Page and Miranda Phillips.

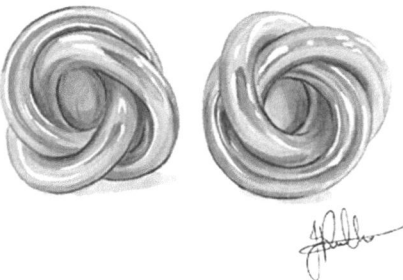

Fig. 9.5 Doula earrings—designed by Jodi Phillips (2018)

diabetes later in life. A doula is conventionally a non-medical person who assists a woman before, during and/or after childbirth, by providing emotional support and physical help if required.[18] Intended to provide similar support digitally, the application logs and presents health data pertaining to the management of diabetes and pregnancy. While other applications provide generic data visualisations that users are required to interpret, Doula provides immediately implementable information to users (e.g., information pertaining to what is safe to eat based on previous entries). The application also includes a community forum that allows women to connect, share stories and reassure one another.

In response to the final outcome, Tamara stated:

Doula is more than just a companion to the earrings; it's a daily companion for women, assisting them in managing their overall health in all aspects of their life and reminding them of the joys of being pregnant.

Implement

Implementation of the wearable technology is still a while away, given the need for regulatory approval. Doula, however, can now assist Glucotek in building a customer base and loyalty, and to secure additional funding from venture capitalists. In this case study design was used to develop a better understanding of Glucotek's position in the digital market, and to

---

[18] Marshall H. Klaus, John H. Kennell, and Phyllis H. Klaus, *The Doula Book: How a Trained Labor Companion Can Help You Have a Shorter, Easier, and Healthier Birth,* 2nd ed. (Cambridge, Massachusetts: Perseus Publishing, 2002).

define a market entry strategy suitable for a forthcoming wearable technology. Given that the technology detailed in this case study is still under development, evaluation is not yet possible. However, metrics for the successful translation of the earrings and application could be captured through public reviews (under platforms such as application stores), and supplemented through feedback from users. Of course, the real metric of success is whether the designs become the industry standard for patients with GDM.

Summarising Doula

Exploring this case study through our framework revealed how design was used to manage the translation of a product undergoing approval. In the process of scaffolding the design of the wearable technology an opportunity in the market was revealed, allowing the start-up to enter the market and build a presence prior to approval of their device. Through the framework, we were able to explore the external and internal conditions of the case, the audit that was conducted, the design intent, the design process and how each order of design was scaffolded, along with a plan for future implementation. This case demonstrates one type of opportunity that can emerge from considering how a design can be scaffolded.

Machines that Keep the Heart Pumping

This case details design initiatives for a Ventricular Assist Device (VAD)—a surgically implanted device used to sustain the circulatory function of a heart in patients with heart failure. These devices can support patients with end stage heart failure while they are awaiting a future donor organ transplant, and are a treatment option for severe, acute, and chronic heart failure.[19] VADs have four key use scenarios:[20]

---

[19] Andrea Montalto, Antonio Loforte, Francesco Musumeci, Thomas Krabatsch, and Mark S. Slaughter, eds. *Mechanical Circulatory Support in End-Stage Heart Failure.* Switzerland: Springer International Publishing, 2017.

[20] Mackenzie Norman Etherington, Keum Hee Kimmi Ko, Jessica Lea Dunn, Karla Straker, Erez Nusem, Cara Wrigley, and Shaun Gregory. "Cascading Mentorship: Designing a Support Tool for Patients with Ventricular Assist Devices." In *Proceedings of DRS 2018 International Conference: Catalyst* , 6:2441–58, 2018.

- to take over (or partially take over) the pumping function of the heart and keep a patient alive while they wait for a donor heart[21]
- to 'buy time' for patients whose condition is unstable or uncertain until a more informed decision regarding the transplant can be made[22]
- to support the heart until it recovers sufficient function for the VAD to be removed without the need for a transplant[23]
- to be implanted as a long-term solution when a patient is not eligible for a transplant.[24]

The invention and implementation of the VAD is the result of over 50 years of collaboration between cardiovascular surgeons, biomedical engineers and immunologists. Collectively, these disciplines designed a pump that would work as efficiently and effectively as possible. Despite the technological and medical achievements the device represents, the external components (e.g. external carry case, batteries, interface, etc.) are bulky. As discussed at the beginning of this book (see p. xi), patients' quality of life following surgery can be far from ideal. Scenarios that can occur in day-to-day use, such as the alarm blaring at inopportune moments, can lead to significant patient distress and dissatisfaction. Evidently, while VADs are a fully functional and implemented device, there remain significant issues that affect patients' and carers' quality of life.[25] The work conducted for this case study was split across a number

---

[21] Bunzel et al., "Mechanical Circulatory Support as a Bridge to Heart Transplantation: What Remains? Long-Term Emotional Sequelae in Patients and Spouses."

[22] Elizabeth A. Ziemba and Ranjit John, "Mechanical Circulatory Support for Bridge to Decision: Which Device and When to Decide," *Journal of Cardiac Surgery* 25, no. 4 (2010): 425–33.

[23] Djordje G Jakovljevic, Magdi H. Yacoub, Stephan Schueler, Guy A. MacGowan, Lazar Velicki, Petar M Seferovic, Sandeep Hothi et al., "Left Ventricular Assist Device as a Bridge to Recovery for Patients With Advanced Heart Failure," *Journal of the American College of Cardiology* 69, no. 15 (2017): 1924–33.

[24] Mehmet C. Oz, Michael Argenziano, Katharine A. Catanese, Michael T. Gardocki, Daniel J. Goldstein, Robert C. Ashton, Annetine C. Gelijns, and Eric A. Rose, "Bridge Experience with Long-Term Implantable Left Ventricular Assist Devices: Are They an Alternative to Transplantation?," *Circulation* 95, no. 7 (1997): 1844–52.

[25] Ko et al., "A Comparative Content Analysis of Digital Channels for Ventricular Assist Device Patients, Caregivers, and Healthcare Practitioners"; Jessica Lea Dunn, Erez Nusem, Karla Straker, Shaun Gregory, and Cara Wrigley, "Human Factors and User Experience Issues with Ventricular Assist Device Wearable Components: A Systematic Review," *Annals of Biomedical Engineering*, 47, no. 12 (2019): 2431–88.

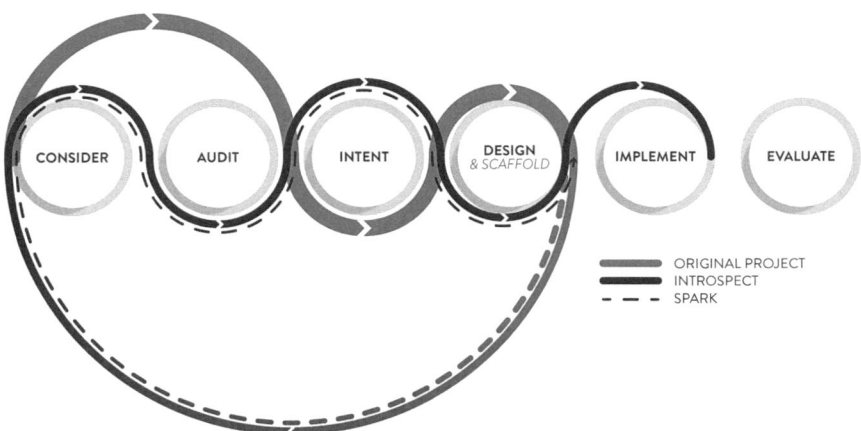

Fig. 9.6 Outline of VAD medical design innovation process

of separate design outputs following the initial stages of the project. Consequently, the framework exhibited for this stream of work is quite divergent (see Fig. 9.6).

Consider

The number of patients awaiting heart transplantation has doubled over the last 15 years,[26] yet only a minor increase in the rate of global heart transplants has been observed.[27] Unfortunately, there are too few donor organs available to meet the demand of patients awaiting heart transplantation.[28] Despite a large market, there is a limited understanding of how circulatory support can be improved beyond the medical research affiliated with the device itself. Current systems have been

---

[26] Anatol Prinzing, Ulf Herold, Anna Berkefeld, Markus Krane, Rüdiger Lange, and Bernhard Voss, "Left Ventricular Assist Devices-Current State and Perspectives," *Journal of Thoracic Disease* 8, no. 8 (2016): E660–66.

[27] Mar Carmona, Marina Álvarez, Jaime Marco, and Beatriz Mahíllo, "Organ Donation and Transplantation Activities 2015 Report," *Global Observatory on Donation and Transplantation (GODT)*, 2017, http://www.transplant-observatory.org/.

[28] Eileen M. Hsich, "Matching the Market for Heart Transplantation Eileen," *Circulation: Heart Failure* 9, no. 4 (2016): e002679.

shown to be unintuitive, requiring better design.[29] Additionally, the role of medical stakeholders as the main point of interaction between a patient and their device is yet to be considered. These stakeholders (caregivers, cardiologists, surgeons and nurses) have the opportunity to improve the experience of, and outcomes for, patients requiring circulatory support. Given the prevalence of VADs, and the host of issues associated with their use, the external conditions are ripe for innovation.

The project outlined in this case study was funded by the Centre for Research Excellence in Advanced Cardio-respiratory Therapies Improving Organ Support (CRE ACTIONS).[30] Due to the challenging experiences of VAD stakeholders, there was appetite for change in a number of hospitals and professional groups Australia-wide. This initiative was therefore not placed within a single entity, but instead represents a multi-disciplinary collaboration between a number of academic and medical institutions. Our team was initially engaged to innovate the device's wearable components to address issues such as: 'power supply', 'wearability and travel freedom', 'the female experience' and 'intuitive handling'.[31] However, discussion with nurses who care for VAD patients also revealed significant strains on medical professionals, which result in compassion fatigue and emotional burnout; nurses spend significant time with these patients and often develop profound relationships, with limited formal support available to help nurses cope when these patients pass away.

Intent

Severe restrictions surrounding the use of the device (e.g. difficulty showering and exercising, a prohibition on swimming, etc.) result in a number of serious issues. Even nurses who care for such patients undergo

---

[29] Etherington et al., "Cascading Mentorship : Designing a Support Tool for Patients with Ventricular Assist Devices."

[30] Grant application number APP1079421 (2014–2019)

[31] Dunn et al., "Human Factors and User Experience Issues with Ventricular Assist Device Wearable Components: A Systematic Review."

challenging experiences, requiring a great deal of emotional resilience.[32] The objective of the design was therefore to empower VAD stakeholders (including patients, caregivers and practitioners).

Design/Scaffold

The research consisted of design projects across three main areas: the device's wearable components (interface, carry pack, battery, alarms, etc.); the services (digital channels such as applications, pre and post operation interactions with family and nurses); and the experience of stakeholders (e.g. preventing infections caused by drivelines). These and other notable components are detailed in Table 9.2.

A number of outputs for design were conceived when initially considering the VAD. These outputs were outside the initial scope for which our team was engaged (i.e., the VAD's external wearable components), but served a significant purpose in empowering VAD stakeholders. Consequently, in this case study we will focus on two designs that were initially 'out of scope', as they illustrate the value of design beyond its

Table 9.2 VAD design outputs

Order	Description
1. Graphic design	'Life-saving device' branding on external battery carry bag to dissuade theft and encourage more careful behaviour around the user
2. Industrial design	Redesign of the device's external components (e.g. carry bag, battery and controller)
3. Interaction design	The design of a digital application for nurses that assists in managing their emotional wellbeing. An application to assist in training carers of VAD patients
4. Systems design	OpenHeart Project (open-source online research platform) to promote collaboration between researchers and laboratories and leverage existing resources and expertise to develop new and improved solutions to improve patient outcomes and quality of life for mechanical circulatory support patients

---

[32] Cara Wrigley, Karla Straker, Erez Nusem, John F. Fraser, Shaun D. Gregory, "Nursing Challenges in Interactions with Patients Receiving Mechanical Circulatory and Respiratory Support," *Journal of Cardiovascular Nursing* 33, no. 5 (2018): E10–15.

obvious applications in medical devices, and highlight how a design can be scaffolded to provide a more considered, holistic experience for stakeholders. The first design output is 'Introspect',[33] a digital intervention to support nurses suffering from compassion fatigue and emotional burnout. The second output is 'Spark', a design that reimagines patient and caregiver training.[34] For clarity, these two design outputs are presented as individual sub-sections.

Introspect: Supporting the Support Person

VAD complications are common, and patients require constant monitoring and considerable attention from nurses while critically ill for extensive periods. Nursing for such patients is complex, multifaceted and intense, with nurses often providing intimate support not only to patients but also to caregivers and family members.[35] Nurses often develop intimate and meaningful relationships with patients due to the nature of their work, yet are offered limited support in dealing with the emotional burden it places upon them (e.g. in the event of a patient passing away).[36]

A support application was therefore designed for nurses, providing a means for nurses to debrief and de-stress through a reflective process.[37] The application provides users a mobile application that facilitates an open and honest conversation with themselves about their emotional state, serving as an opportunity to promote, maintain and nurture positive mental health practices in a private manner.

---

[33] Introspect was designed by Natalia Gulbransen-diaz, Ling Yi Feng and Rachel Montgomery.

[34] Spark was designed by Mackenzie Etherington. For more information on Spark see https://www.mackenziee.com/spark/.

[35] Wrigley et al., "Nursing Challenges in Interactions with Patients Receiving Mechanical Circulatory and Respiratory Support."

[36] Wrigley et al.

[37] For more information on the application see https://youtu.be/o-FpaTbejHU.

Consider

Nurses of VAD patients face a number of complex emotional challenges, with their role being defined by caring and supporting not only patients, but also their families and caregivers. Along with ethical and emotional demands, nurses feel responsible to provide compassion and support. The constant demands of the job (namely being patient-centric and patient advocates) result in a number of multifaceted emotional challenges. These challenges are often defined as compassion fatigue,[38] and characterised by overexposure to trauma in nursing work (such as witnessing patient suffering or taking on patient suffering vicariously). Such factors can hinder nurses' capacity to engage in genuine empathy or connection.

As a field mental health is increasing in prominence and receiving attention. Furthermore, the value of supporting our support people is being more widely accepted. As supporting nurses doesn't necessitate a formal medical intervention, it may be possible to circumvent regulatory bodies and design an output that is open-access. For these reasons, it can be stated that an appropriate design would be well-received and garner external support.

Audit

Preliminary research consisted of a series of focus groups that aimed to provide an in-depth qualitative perspective on the challenges nurses face when caring for VAD patients.[39] The challenges explored ranged across three topics synthesised from the literature (i.e. exclusive knowledge, patient relationships and compassion fatigue). The methodological basis for the study was interpretive phenomenological analysis—an approach to qualitative analysis that focuses on how people make sense of

---

[38] Carla Joinson, "Coping with Compassion Fatigue," *Nursing* 22, no. 4 (1992): 116, 118–19, 120; Siedine Knobloch Coetzee and Hester C. Klopper, "Compassion Fatigue within Nursing Practice: A Concept Analysis," *Nursing & Health Sciences* 12, no. 2 (2010): 235–43.

[39] Wrigley et al., "Nursing Challenges in Interactions with Patients Receiving Mechanical Circulatory and Respiratory Support."

their experiences.[40] Analysis revealed that future designs should assist nurses in being aware of and maintaining their emotional state; communicating information to the right people at appropriate times; enabling directed help or intervention when required; and integration of these factors into their daily routine.

The challenges explored in the research are not exclusive to nurses in this field, and could affect any nursing practitioner. Thus, the subsequent research was extended to include the perspectives of other nurses in high-stress wards (such as emergency, drug health and oncology) and graduate nurses who lack support and experience from colleagues. A set of semi-structured interviews was therefore conducted to investigate:

- obstacles and frustrations in the nursing profession
- emotional strategies utilised by nurses to cope with emotional challenges
- sources of alleviation for emotional challenges.

Findings were used to develop more thorough understandings of how nurses cope with emotional challenges. While most strategies and techniques were found to be constructive, some sources of relief (such as alcohol consumption) were recognised to have damaging consequences for nurses' health. In particular, the interviews highlighted the potential for digital interventions in this space. Mobile health applications, in particular, are capable of measuring, monitoring and interpreting increasingly complex health data,[41] and thus have increasing potential as platforms that support health.

The next stage of research was a content analysis to identify trends in digital mental health interventions. Interventions were charted according

[40] Michael Larkin and Andrew Thompson, "Interpretative Phenomenological Analysis in Mental Health and Psychotherapy Research," in *Qualitative Research Methods in Mental Health and Psychotherapy: A Guide for Students and Practitioners*, ed. A. Thompson and D. Harper (Oxford: John Wiley & Sons, 2012), 99–116.

[41] Thyra de Jongh, Ipek Gurol-Urganci, Vlasta Vodopivec-Jamsek, Josip Car, and Rifat Atun, "Mobile Phone Messaging for Facilitating Self-Management of Long-Term Illnesses," *Cochrane Database of Systematic Reviews* 12 (2012); Maddalena Fiordelli, Nicola Diviani, and Peter J. Schulz, "Mapping MHealth Research: A Decade of Evolution," *Journal of Medical Internet Research* 15, no. 5 (2013): e95.

to their purpose (from general mental wellbeing support to more specialised uses) and their reliance on external input (such as professional psychological guidance or the requirement of independent engagement). Three typologies were identified to encompass applications' contents.

Analysis of the market revealed a significant oversaturation of interventions for general mental wellbeing, consisting of applications that featured learning modules focused on educational content and raising awareness. These corresponded poorly to nurses' need for accessible, private interventions that provide a platform for emotional processing and relief (as identified in the semi-structured interviews). While such applications had a positive correlation to general wellbeing, their indirect and unfocused nature hindered their capacity to address specific emotional distresses. Notably, it was found that most interventions focused on pilot programs and technological development rather than stakeholders' needs, and market acceptance and adoption.

Intent

Insights gathered in preliminary stages revealed that nurses are adversely affected by the emotional costs of their profession, yet are not sufficiently supported or equipped to deal with these challenges. It was determined that the proposed design should therefore promote, nurture and provide nurses with positive and healthy mental health practices; empowering them in the face of adversity.

Design/Scaffold

In line with human-centred design approaches, the designers first gained an understanding of the problem space.[42] This phase was detailed in the audit, with key findings used to inform a rapid ideation phase and the initial concept. The concept (see Fig. 9.7), Introspect, prompts the user with carefully formulated questions to create a dialogue for reflection and introspection, and promotes positive mental health practices.

---

[42] Brown, "Design Thinking."

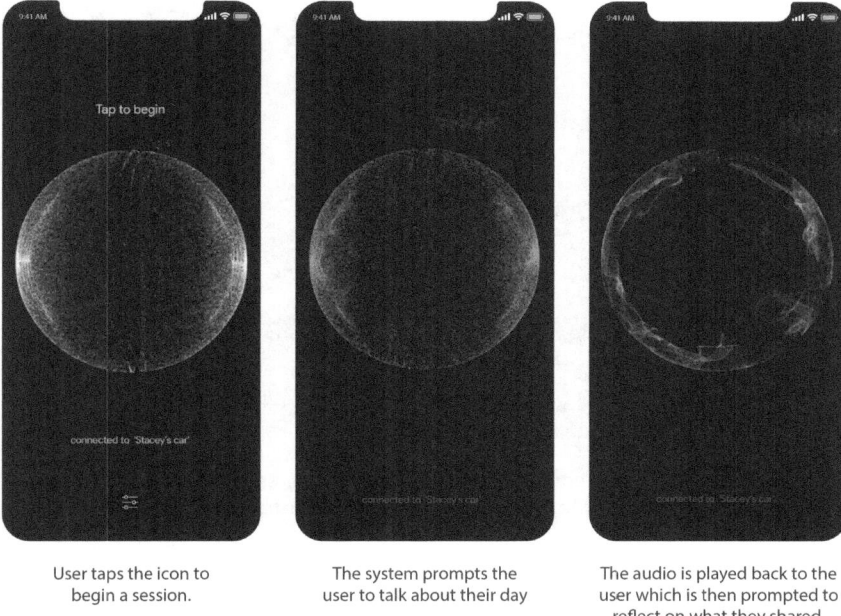

| User taps the icon to begin a session. | The system prompts the user to talk about their day | The audio is played back to the user which is then prompted to reflect on what they shared. |

Fig. 9.7 Introspect application—designed by Natalia Gulbransen-diaz, Ling Yi Feng and Rachel Montgomery

The audio-based self-care intervention aims to help nurses support positive mental health practices. Conversations with the system encourage nurses to talk about and reflect on their feelings, in order to help in processing them. The system unpacks a nurse's emotional state by prompting them: 'tell me about your day'. When a response is received, the audio is played back to the user in a modulated tone before the system asks the user 'having heard that back, what are you thinking?' Introspect can be privately and independently used for as long or as little as a user chooses.

The concept was tested using a simulated-contextual walkthrough that engaged twelve participants (registered nurses and academics with extensive clinical experience) to ascertain perceptions of the concept. The researchers simulated the experience of driving in a vehicle, as they believed the prototype would most likely be used in this scenario (Fig. 9.8

Monitor displaying dash-cam footage to simualte the driving experience

Speakers

Digital prototype displayed on a phone, placed with a phone holder

Cardboard steering wheel

Voice recorder

Fig. 9.8 Simulated-contextual walkthrough testing environment (courtesy of Natalia Gulbransen-diaz, Ling Yi Feng and Rachel Montgomery)

depicts the space in which testing was conducted). A monitor showing late-night dash-cam footage was set up to emulate the experience of driving, and a cardboard steering wheel provided additional immersion. The prototype was hosted on a mobile phone placed in a device holder at eye level and served as a more detailed representation of the design. This method of contextual simulation, which is unique to laboratory testing, presented a set of distinct advantages: it replicated the familiar setting to increase participant comfort; imitated a realistic use-case scenario; and provided designers with in-situ opportunities to identify problems in both the interface and the experience.

Data were captured through semi-structured interviews during the usability testing, with interviews exploring the users' experience with the concept. Participants noted that the design allowed them to find closure; increased awareness of their emotions and thoughts; and enabled them to reconsider situations in a new light and reframe their perspectives. These findings served as preliminary validation of the concept and the strategies it employed (namely vocalisation and reflection).

Implement

While the design is undergoing final testing, implementation is anticipated to take place across three phases. First, alpha testing and release for selected nursing departments. Second, beta testing in other healthcare contexts and high-stress professions. Thirdly, open access to the general public. This research is driven by the hope of providing real benefits to nurses, the healthcare industry and broader society. We hope that an accessible, digital intervention engaging nurses in positive mental health practices will assist in increasing nurse retention and provide additional support to those who care for us.

Spark: Training to Empower Patients

A VAD (see Fig. 9.9) consists of a core component implanted within the body, and a number of wearable components through which users interact with the device.[43] Managing these components, and the VAD itself, requires users to navigate several complex interfaces and procedures. For instance, users must be able to comfortably interact with the monitor

Fig. 9.9 VAD and controller (courtesy of Mackenzie Etherington)

---

[43] Thomas Schloglhofer and Heinrich Schima, "Wearable Systems," in *Mechanical Circulatory and Respiratory Support*, ed. Shaun D Gregory, Michael C Stevens, and John F Fraser (New York: Elsevier, 2018), 691–721.

providing information on the performance of the device, diagnostic data, battery charge, pump function and safety alarms. Another persistent concern is driveline infections. The exit site of the driveline—a cable running through a patient's abdomen which connects the implanted device to the external components—requires a strict management routine to avoid infection and inflammation. This includes daily cleaning, regular dressing changes and inspection to ensure the wound remains uncontaminated.[44]

The design of the VAD's external components must therefore provide "absolutely fail-safe function",[45] yet many human factors and user experience issues remain.[46] To address these pervasive challenges, two primary strategies have been adopted. First, a design for the external, wearable components (i.e. the batteries and controller) that caters to the numerous user groups that interact with them. Specifically, a design that is that is sufficiently intuitive for novice users to be capable of providing aid in an emergency. Second, ensuring the correct use of these components through patient and caregiver training and exercise interventions.[47] These two approaches have merit but fail to holistically consider a key stakeholder: the caregiver.

Consider

Patients and caregivers begin their training and exercise interventions before the VAD is implanted, and continue their training in hospital following their surgery.[48] Part of the discharge process in some hospitals requires patients to demonstrate their understanding of basic VAD skills

---

[44] Yue Qu et al., "Percutaneous and Transcutaneous Connections," in *Mechanical Circulatory and Respiratory Support*, ed. Shaun D Gregory, Michael C Stevens, and John F Fraser (New York: Elsevier, 2018), 659–89.

[45] Schloglhofer and Schima, "Wearable Systems," 691.

[46] Jessica Lea Dunn et al., "Human Factors and User Experience Issues with Ventricular Assist Device Wearable Components: A Systematic Review," *Annals of Biomedical Engineering*, July 2019.

[47] Cynthia M Dougherty and Ana Carolina Sauer Liberato, "A Systematic Review of Exercise Training in Cardiac Implantable Devices (CID)S," *Circulation* 138, no. A10413 (2018).

[48] Joseph A. R. Englert, Jennifer A. Davis, and Selim R. Krim, "Mechanical Circulatory Support for the Failing Heart: Continuous-Flow Left Ventricular Assist Devices," *The Ochsner Journal* 16(3) (2016): 263–69.

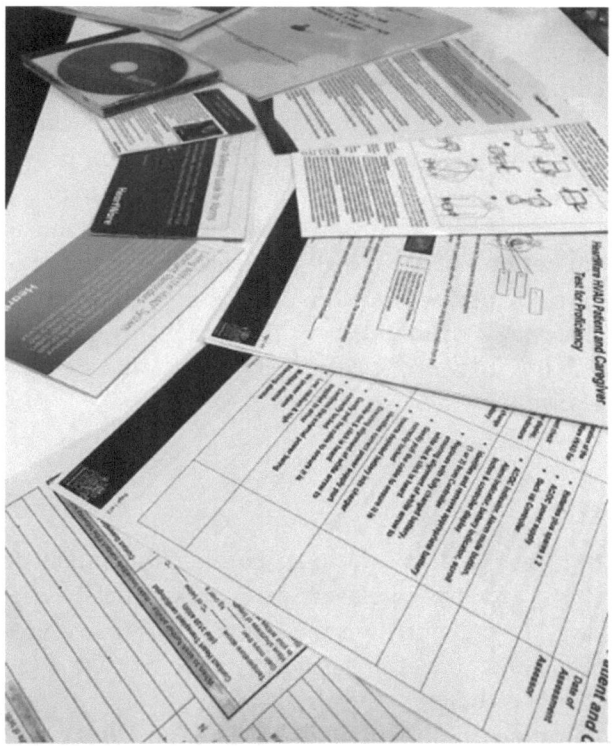

Fig. 9.10 VAD information pack and essentials (courtesy of Mackenzie Etherington)

(e.g. bathing and dressing with a VAD, changing battery packs, identifying alarms and vibrations, and using supportive gear for wearing the device)[49] and the daily driveline care routine.[50] Information packs (see Fig. 9.10) are also provided to patients and caregivers. The contents of these packs vary between hospitals and VAD manufactures.[51]

---

[49] Dorthe Overgaard, Heidi Grufstedt Kjeldgaard, and Ingrid Egerod, "Life in Transition: A Qualitative Study of the Illness Experience and Vocational Adjustment of Patients With Left Ventricular Assist Device," *Journal of Cardiovascular Nursing* 27, no. 5 (2012): 394–402.

[50] Martha Abshire et al., "Adaptation and Coping in Patients Living with an LVAD: A Meta Synthesis," *Heart & Lung* 45, no. 5 (n.d.): 397–405.

[51] Mackenzie Norman Etherington et al., "Cascading Mentorship: Designing a Support Tool for Patients with Ventricular Assist Devices," in *Proceedings of DRS 2018 International Conference: Catalyst*, vol. 6, 2018, 2441–58.

Learning basic VAD skills while in hospital is overwhelming for many patients,[52] resulting in the caregiver being required to 'master' these skills. It is expected that the patient will then develop these skills later on.[53] However, studies have highlighted that patients and caregivers often struggle with the overwhelming amount of information provided, resulting in psychosocial issues in the form of increased anxiety and fear.[54] Furthermore, caregivers wanting to know how to respond to an alarm would have to either correctly recall the relevant procedure or find it in the information pack provided. Both options are extremely stressful during an emergency. We surmised that simplifying this training and better integrating the training into stakeholders' lives could help patients and caregivers to surmount these challenges.

Audit

To understand the available solutions, 16 digital channels designed for VAD users (i.e., patients, caregivers and practitioners) were identified and analysed.[55] A content analysis methodology[56] was employed to analyse the purpose, interactivity, features, functionality, information and focus of each digital channel. The results from this study highlighted that a mobile application could reduce the burden on VAD stakeholders by enabling direct communication channels and remote self-management. Long-term, these engagements could benefit users by reducing the risk of

[52] Claire Hallas, Nicholas R. Banner, and Jo Wray, "A Qualitative Study of the Psychological Experience of Patients During and After Mechanical Cardiac Support," *The Journal of Cardiovascular Nursing* 24, no. 1 (2009): 31–39, https://doi.org/10.1097/01.JCN.0000317472.65671.e2.

[53] Jesus M Casida et al., "Lifestyle Adjustments of Adults with Long-Term Implantable Left Ventricular Assist Devices: A Phenomenologic Inquiry," *Heart & Lung* 40, no. 6 (2011): 511–20.

[54] Elizabeth Chapman et al., "Psychosocial Issues for Patients with Ventricular Assist Devices: A Qualitative Pilot Study." *American Journal of Critical Care : An Official Publication, American Association of Critical-Care Nurses* 16, no. 1 (2007): 72–81; Ottenberg et al., "Choices for Patients 'Without a Choice' Interviews With Patients Who Received a Left Ventricular Assist Device as Destination Therapy."

[55] Keum Hee Kimmi Ko et al., "A Comparative Content Analysis of Digital Channels for Ventricular Assist Device Patients, Caregivers, and Healthcare Practitioners," *American Society of Artificial Internal Organs* 65, no. 8 (2019): 855–63.

[56] Satu Elo and Helvi Kyngäs, "The Qualitative Content Analysis Process," *Journal of Advanced Nursing* 62, no. 1 (2008): 107–15.

known challenges (e.g. driveline infections) by providing early detection and treatment.[57] In a content analysis study which analysed the strengths and weaknesses of three VAD mobile applications, the following limitations were found:[58]

- Lack of 'real-time' access to healthcare professionals
- Unintuitive interfaces (e.g. illogical placement of menu items)
- Casual communication of confronting content (e.g. morality, negative health results)

Intent

Each VAD patient requires a caregiver. It can be as challenging, if not more so, for a caregiver to adapt to the lifestyle impacts of the VAD treatment than it is for the patient. The insights obtained from the consider and audit stages highlighted that current training processes and resources were developed for the VAD patient, yet the caregiver was the one responsible for implementing the training. This informed the intent: to train caregivers to support VAD patients. Given that intent was framed around the patient and was reactive through its response to an existing issue, the intended outcome can be defined as empowerment.

Design/Scaffold

The first stage in the design process was to understand the current VAD user experience. A literature review was conducted to identify the key pain points in the user journey. These pain points were subsequently translated into user requirements through personas,[59] journey maps and

---

[57] Ko et al., "A Comparative Content Analysis of Digital Channels for Ventricular Assist Device Patients, Caregivers, and Healthcare Practitioners."

[58] Etherington et al., "Cascading Mentorship: Designing a Support Tool for Patients with Ventricular Assist Devices."

[59] Personas are archetypal representations of the target stakeholders that are formed out of the insights and themes uncovered from user research.

affinity diagramming;[60] a set of design tools used to stimulate empathy.[61] Insights emerging from this process informed a design brief and the solution requirements, thus ensuring that the design would accommodate the identified user needs.

Particularly of note, and the key focus of the design, was the requirement to make the identification of different VAD alarms in emergency scenarios easier. The design also needed to accommodate psychological aspects such as emotional burden that were found to influence the caregiver's process of learning to use a VAD and its monitor.[62] In addition, this process identified three key user needs for patients and caregivers:

- The need to feel confident in their ability to deal with situations as they arise
- The need to trust information provided
- The need to feel prepared and in control

A mobile application was developed to address these issues and user needs (see Fig. 9.11). The application primarily focused on the caregiver and ensured that training would occur from the very start of the VAD journey. This would equip a caregiver with the skills to help train the patient once discharged from hospital.

Several interface designs were developed for user testing and to explore usability during common tasks such as onboarding (setting up a profile) and other quick lessons. The quick lessons focused on the identification of different alarms and learning what actions are required during each type of emergency scenario. These lessons were designed to allow easy access to information, and promote learnt behaviours through repeatable actions to empower users with the knowledge to respond in an emergency. For example, through tasks involving the identification of different alarms. Given this was effectively a simulation, a tangible connection between the mobile application and a wearable device was developed (see

---

[60] Affinity diagramming is a process that refines and synthesises a broad range of user data from various research methods into clear patterns and groupings.

[61] Etherington et al., "Cascading Mentorship: Designing a Support Tool for Patients with Ventricular Assist Devices."

[62] For more information on these insights, see Etherington et al.

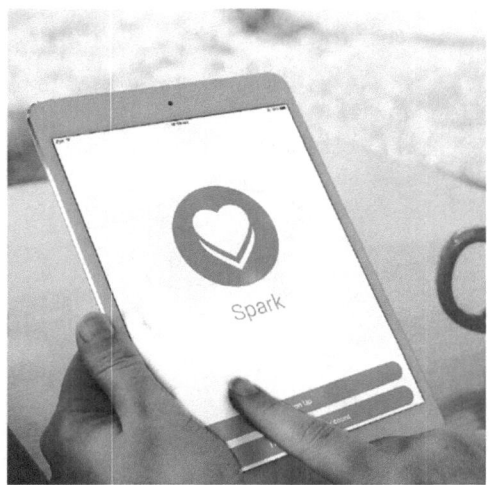 

Fig. 9.11 Spark training solution—designed by Mackenzie Etherington

Fig. 9.12) to replicate the experience of interacting with a wearable device (such as the VAD).

User testing also highlighted a number of other design opportunities. Notably, one VAD caregiver expressed a desire for fewer face-to-face visits with health practitioner to check for driveline infections. An in-app remote monitoring solution was therefore developed, allowing users to send a photo of the driveline exit site to their physician so that potential infections could be diagnosed (Fig. 9.13). Thus, reducing the need for face-to-face visits and providing patients and caregivers greater autonomy.

The intent of Spark was to empower VAD caregivers and patients by equipping them with the skills to better manage life with a VAD. Features like remote monitoring and quick lessons were designed to assist VAD caregivers and patients to be less burdened by the VAD, and to build their confidence and ability to recall vital information during emergencies. An integrated wearable component was used to build contextual empathy for caregivers (simulating the experience of wearing and interacting with the VAD controller) and provide authenticity to the experience created by the design. This case

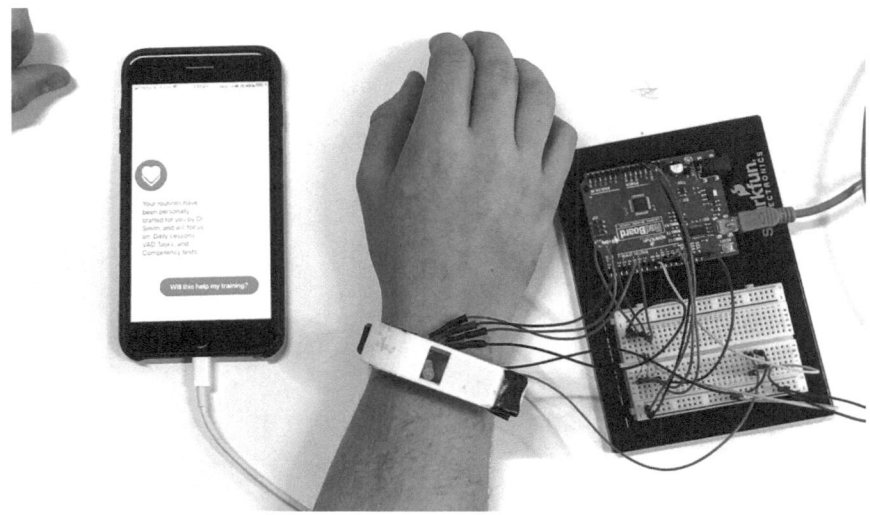

Fig. 9.12 Spark application and wearable prototype—designed by Mackenzie Etherington

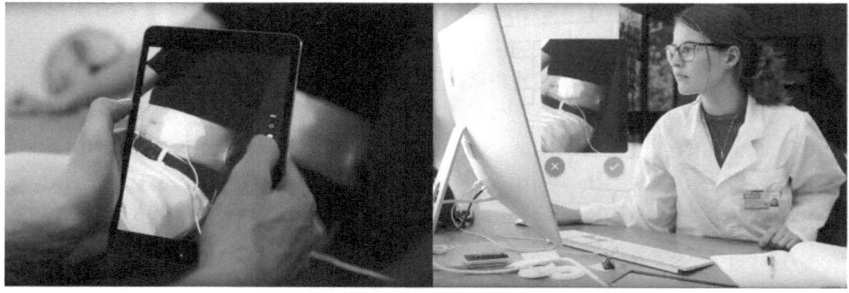

Fig. 9.13 Diagnosis simulation with physician—designed by Mackenzie Etherington

study demonstrates that, even for immaculately designed life-saving devices, a simple interaction design can have tremendous impact on stakeholders' quality of life.

Summarising Introspect and Spark

In exploring the designs of Introspect and Spark we discuss the numerous directions available for design when supporting an existing medical device. Our focus here was to demonstrate that even fully implemented medical devices can benefit from design in the form of scaffolding. Scaffolding can reveal opportunities (some of which are relatively easy to implement) that have little to do with the medical device itself, yet can be of significant benefit to patients, caregivers and medical stakeholders. To identify such opportunities, all that's required is to observe and ask.

*   *   *

In Chaps. 8 and 9 we have focused on 'design', introducing the medical design innovation framework in further detail and illustrating its application through three case studies facilitated by the authors. In our selection of these cases we hoped to convey that design in health and medicine doesn't always have to be grand, expensive or revolutionary. Indeed, even the simplest interventions can have significant impact. Furthermore, we highlighted three major considerations for design that remain nascent in the literature.

First, the need to consider the scope of design. The magnitude of design is growing, and managing a larger scope sometimes necessitates more than the ambitions of a single entity or organisation. As demonstrated by the Bravo case study, organisations or practitioners seeking to drive industry-wide change should consider soliciting aid from their peers and incorporating others in their initiatives. It is challenging for one catalyst to pave the way. Collectively, we can create meaningful change.

Second, design can be of significant value while undergoing lengthy approval for medical devices. Doula illustrated how design could be used to conceive alternative pathways for market penetration that can serve as a source of revenue, and a means for developing a brand and reputation prior to the launch of a primary product or service. In the case of Doula we demonstrate how a digital application can be an excellent way to build a brand and capture a segment of the market while waiting for a medical device to be approved by regulatory bodies.

Third, properly scaffolding a design can have a major impact on success, and on stakeholders' quality of life. There is potential for design beyond state-of-the-art medical devices. Many medical devices are revolutionary, allowing us to tackle complex medical challenges that were previously beyond our scope. However, our ability to create positive medical experiences has not developed at the same rate. The experience of life with a VAD, for example, leaves much to be desired by patients, caregivers and nurses.

A plethora of opportunities remain for design—even when considering the lengthy approval and launch times for medical devices and services, some of which are relatively easy to realise and implement and can have significant value despite their simplicity. Through Introspect and Spark we demonstrate how the disciplines of design can be used to scaffold a medical device and address the deficits of some medical interventions.

We hope that through these examples we are able to illustrate a number of opportunities for design in health and medicine, and that practitioners are able to use our framework as a means of building *capacity* in the medical sector, developing *knowledge* within our society, *enabling* our medical professionals and *empowering* patients.

10

Implementing Design in Health and Medicine

This book began with the quote 'Medicine can treat the disease; great medicine treats the patient who has the disease'.[1] In Part I of the book we highlighted four distinct outcomes (*capacity, knowledge, enablement* and *empowerment*) to frame the ways in which design innovation can create 'great medical design'. In exploring these outcomes, we demonstrated the value offered by design (in its many forms), of considering the experiences of patients and clinicians, and of ensuring that healthcare is not transactional and impersonal. In Part II we introduced the medical design innovation framework as a means of assisting practitioners to address medical opportunities and challenges through design. In this final chapter we propose a set of design principles and actions that elaborate further on how a design can be transitioned from a concept to practice. We hope that these final considerations will serve as tangible guidelines for those seeking to practise design in health and medicine.

Design is not just about following a process. Certain principles and actions (considered throughout a design process) can make the difference between success and failure. We have therefore synthesised insights from

---

[1] Based on Sir William Osler's quote 'The good physician treats the disease; the great physician treats the patient who has the disease'.

© The Author(s) 2020
E. Nusem et al., *Design Innovation for Health and Medicine*,
https://doi.org/10.1007/978-981-15-4362-3_10

Parts I and II and derived them into a set of principles and actions. These can assist designers to overcome common pitfalls and to best leverage their resources and findings. These principles and actions are presented across three key areas: frame intent, leverage design and plan implementation.

Frame Intent

Design shouldn't be practiced 'purely for the sake of it'. Too often is design poorly considered, resulting in an application that no one wants, or a product that no one will use. Prior to designing, it is important to understand *why* design is being engaged. An objective or an aim for design is integral for ensuring that design will create the right outcomes. Three major components which factor into creating the right outcomes are: solving the right problem(s), defining the scope of design and developing metrics for success. These components are further detailed in Table 10.1.

Leverage Design

Familiarity with, or the convenience of, a certain order of design can influence which mode of design is selected to address a given problem or opportunity. However, these factors are poor determinants for the selection of an order of design. The order of design selected must be equal to the challenge at hand in order to ensure that the desired outcomes are achieved. Often, this necessities contributions from a number of the orders. Furthermore, the activities undertaken throughout the design process should adequately engage key stakeholders to ensure that any consequent solution addresses their needs, and that there is sufficient support to adopt the design following implementation. The principles and actions that comprise this area are detailed in Table 10.2.

Table 10.1 Principles and actions for framing intent

Principle	Description	Actions
Solve the right problem(s)	When addressing a problem, it is important to focus on the root cause rather than the symptoms. Without a proper understanding of the problem at hand, it is all too easy to develop a 'band-aid solution' which does little to address the underlying issue(s). This necessitates understanding the larger issues at play along with their intricacies	• Identify primary and secondary problems for the various stakeholders • Consider clinicians, patients, carers, the context of design and any other outliers • Understand interactions between all stakeholders and entities involved (e.g. clinicians, patients and the context)
Define the scope of design	Design is subject to a range of complications that span beyond the design itself. For example, aspects (such as social stigma) could hinder the adoption of a product or service. These aspects should be considered as part of the design process and be accounted for within the final design outcome	• Consider the full road-map for design (from conceptualisation to implementation) • Develop insights into industry trends and future direction(s) • Investigate potential utilisation of emerging technologies and trends
Develop metrics for success	Determining the success of design is challenging without appropriate metrics for measuring the outcomes. Developing appropriate metrics (including long-term and short-term objectives and goals) is therefore an integral component for ensuring that the appropriate outcomes are created. Such metrics can also help to establish whether the intended outcomes of design have been met, and to define any future activities required to assist in meeting these outcomes	• Define the purpose and value of the solution • Determine the desired outcomes • Incorporate means of measuring user experience • Consider if the solution will continue to create value in the future (e.g. in five, ten, fifteen or twenty years)

Table 10.2 Principles and actions for leveraging design

Principle	Description	Actions
Oscillate between the orders	Design encompasses a number of disciplines, and most applications of design can benefit from a number of these. When designing it is important not only to select the right order of design, but to also consider how the orders can be jointly used to create the best outcomes. For example, when designing a product, it is pivotal to also consider the system in which the product would exist	• Question whether the intended order of design has been selected for the right reasons • Maintain awareness of the process and how each order of design could be used as a scaffold • Actively consider which orders of design are relevant for each component at every stage of the design process
Design with stakeholders	In design it is important to consider all stakeholders' perspectives when exploring a problem and/or solution. This is best accomplished by practicing empathy and engaging with stakeholders (through methods such as co-design) to capture primary data. Start by observing everything in the context of study, not just the people or products	• Engage users as active participants in design • Question what is not working well in the current environment and why • Put yourself in the shoes of the patient (e.g. lie in bed for hours listening to the sounds of machines, wear hospital gowns, speak to nurses, attempt wayfinding in a wheelchair) • Explore inconsistencies between what people say and do

Plan Implementation

Design isn't just about creating concepts, guidelines and recommendations. It's about creating something tangible and implementable. Most individuals are quite capable of coming up with a good idea, yet turning an idea into a reality is an entirely different story. Developing a roadmap for implementation is something which can be easily overlooked, yet is an integral component of design. Implementation is a broad and complex subject, which could alone fill the contents of a book. Unfortunately, given the range of implementation strategies and their variations based on the context of each design, we were unable to explore implementation comprehensively within this manuscript. Nevertheless, the principles and actions detailed in Table 10.3 should provide a starting point for practitioners considering how to prepare a design for implementation.

Table 10.3 Principles and actions for planning implementation

Principle	Description	Actions
Engage the right stakeholders	Design requires support and engagement from a wide range of stakeholders. Ensuring that these stakeholders are involved and invested in the success of the design from early stages can be paramount to success. Internally (i.e. within an organisation), this can ensure that buy-in and support are generated. Externally (e.g. with regulatory bodies and policymakers), this can ensure that constraints are not overlooked	• Engage key stakeholders early and be inclusive • Articulate purpose, timelines, goals and risks • Use effective methods of communication (e.g. graphic design) • Think about how the design can be supported within existing systems • Consider the regulations or policies that may inhibit implementation of the proposed design solution

(*continued*)

Table 10.3 (continued)

Principle	Description	Actions
Plan for market entry, growth and scaling	A key consideration of design is whether a proposed solution will be accepted amongst clinicians, carers and patients. This occurs not only during market entry, but also as an organisation grows and its products mature. The scale and growth[a] strategy of the organisation is crucial in the implementation strategy, as scaling too fast, no matter how brilliant the idea, can result in a market failure	• Consider market attractiveness, distribution channel identification, intellectual property protection, and launch strategy • Also consider human elements such as market adoption and uptake, and stakeholder buy–in (e.g. clinicians prescribing the application, and the training of clinical staff on a new system, product or protocol)
Develop environments in which design can thrive	Design requires appropriate spaces to flourish. For example, design hubs provide a space for innovation activities to occur, and for hosting external stakeholders to capture or share insights. Likewise, living labs and prototyping spaces can provide an in-situ location close to relevant stakeholders for testing ideas and attaining feedback rapidly. These are a critical aspect of implementation as they provide an avenue for generating buy-in and feedback	• Determine likely hurdles for implementation and attain appropriate spaces to overcome these • Have presence in highly visible spaces to provide transparency for the design work being conducted • Create open and accessible environments for stakeholders to engage with, and be informed by, design

[a]Growing a business means adding resources at about the same rate that revenue is created. Scaling, however, means adding resources at an incremental rate while creating revenue at an exponential rate

Final Thoughts

As our society becomes more interconnected and developed, so too do our problems. It is no wonder that then, the role of the designer must change and adapt to face these emerging challenges. Indeed, we are living longer than ever before,[2] and facing issues (such as mass environmental change, social inequity, pandemics and globalisation) that place incredible strain on our health systems and global resources. This book presents design as a method of addressing such challenges, allowing us to manage ambiguity in complex situations. In addition, through design we are able to holistically understand the needs of patients and clinicians, and how to create optimal outcomes in health and medicine.

However, we must recognise that design is not the answer to all problems. Understanding the multifaceted field of health care and the plethora of variables that are often overlooked in the product development process is also of pivotal importance. As demonstrated by the medical design innovation framework described in this book, it is important to: understand the conditions in which we design; gain insight into latent needs of our stakeholders and the state of the market through audits; define our intent and the outcomes we wish to create; design holistically and determine how to best scaffold our design outputs; and to implement and evaluate our contributions. These elements, if not considered collectively, result in ideas that fail to translate into tangible outcomes; ideas alone cannot save or improve lives.

In Part I of the book we illustrated design innovation in health and medicine through a number of case studies. The cases serve to demonstrate the applications of design in health and medicine, along with how design can be used and the outcomes it can create in this context. It is important to keep in mind Maslow's famous analogy that if all you have is a hammer, everything looks like a nail. Indeed, many design initiatives begin with an assumption of what needs to be designed, rather than starting with understanding the problem being addressed and the outcomes that should be achieved. Only once the problem and stakeholders (e.g. patients, carers, families and medical practitioners) are understood can we begin to realise and achieve our intent. We elaborate on this

---

[2] This is evident as this is the oldest you have ever been.

malpractice, and on the need for design in health care to be multi-disciplinary, collaborative and well-reasoned.

Part II described the primary case studies on which this book is founded. In describing these cases we model the medical design innovation framework—an iterative design process that assists in translating a concept into tangible outcomes in health care. This framework was conceived through our collaborations with medical engineers and clinicians as a means of bridging the gap from idea to implementation. There is a breadth of literature that justifies the use of design to attain market acceptance for medical devices in the conception of a project, yet the applications of design in the translation of a concept are often overlooked. Indeed, solutions must make it to market for patient and practitioner outcomes to be realised.

Design innovation for health and medicine is a rapidly growing field, with increasing recognition in both practice and academia. A number of medical design research groups have been established to explore the various intersections of these two disciplines through ground-breaking partnerships. While there is still much to learn about these intersections, our objective in writing this book is to share the knowledge and findings from our collaborations and research. We hope that design can be thought of as more than a thinking exercise, but as a means of creating medical outcomes that improve the lives of practitioners, patients and their loved ones.

Appendix: Case Study Summaries

Table A.1 3D Printing summary

Case study	3D printing: customised solution to assistive tools (p. 61)
Intent	Design for enablement
Typology	Procedural instruments
User	Medical practitioners and patients requiring implants
Unmet needs	Customisable medical implants for surgery and tailored anatomical models for surgical practice
Context	Using 'off-the-shelf solution' implants can lead to issues and complications for patients
Insight	• Generic implants are often ill-suited to patients resulting in poor medical outcomes
	• Practising on 3D printed models of patients' organs can reduce surgery time and trauma caused to patients
	• 3D printing in medicine can provide rapid access to sterile surgical instruments and implants, and produce customisable solutions in a range of contexts
	• Cost of 3D printing can be significantly lower than traditional manufacturing for custom devices
Aim	Provide customisable implants and models to assist in surgery preparation, and reduce risk of implant rejection or failure and surgery time
Design outcome	Access to patient-specific 3D printed implants and anatomic training models

© The Author(s) 2020
E. Nusem et al., *Design Innovation for Health and Medicine*,
https://doi.org/10.1007/978-981-15-4362-3

Table A.2   Cochlear summary

Case study	Cochlear: ensuring everyone can hear (p. 77)
Intent	Design for empowerment
Typology	Promoting ability
User	People suffering hearing loss
Unmet needs	Holistic hearing experience for individuals suffering from hearing loss
Context	Continuing to understand how the ear works and provide solutions for patient needs and desires
Insight	• Stimulating the inner ear with electrodes can restore hearing • Multi-channel stimulation can allow patients to understand speech • Community and experience are an integral aspect of addressing hearing-impairment
Aim	Transform the way people understand and treat hearing loss
Design outcome	Cochlear implanted device restores hearing while the Cochlear community provides support through rehabilitation, access to industry experts, device service and repairs

Table A.3   Concrn summary

Case study	Concrn: alternative support for the homeless (p. 26)
Intent	Design for capacity
Typology	Information systems
User	Mentally ill and homeless people in San Francisco
Unmet needs	Empathetic means for supporting homeless and mentally ill people in distress
Context	80% of calls per month to the San Francisco Police were related to mental health
Insight	• Police calls relating to the homeless often resulted in hospital admission, however, hospitals have limited capacity to assist resulting in swift discharge back onto the streets • Police and hospital intervention can be inappropriate responses to mental health situations and emergencies • Adequate support includes listening to distressed individuals' needs, helping calm them and providing referrals to services
Aim	Provide appropriate channels for supporting and engaging distressed homeless and mentally ill people
Design outcome	Mobile application that acts as a 911 alternative for individuals suffering from mental illness and homelessness

Table A.4 CT scanner summary

Case study	CT scanners: an ambient experience (p. 34)
Intent	Design for capacity
Typology	Efficiency innovations
User	Children undergoing a CT scan
Unmet needs	Constructive experience for children undergoing a CT scan
Context	CT scans require patients to remain still yet offer no mechanisms to assist with this
Insight	• Developments in CT scanners were mainly for the benefit of radiographers (improvements in quality of images, reduction in duration of the procedure, reduction in cost) • Patients (children in particular) are often anxious during scans and struggle to remain still, and are therefore exposed to additional radiation and sometimes require sedation
Aim	Create an experience that would assist child patients to stay still, thereby reducing the amount of radiation exposure and sedations required
Design outcome	Customisable 'ambient experience' which immerses the child in a story and encourages them to stay still throughout the CT scan

Table A.5 Drones summary

Case study	Drones: rapid response aids (p. 29)
Intent	Design for capacity
Typology	System automation
User	Medical stakeholders in remote or difficult to reach locations
Unmet needs	Timely access to medical aid and medication
Context	Due to geographical, landscape and infrastructure constraints health practitioners sometimes do not have the timely access required to deliver medical aid to patients
Insight	• Automation of services can result in more timely responses to medical emergencies • Centralising supply can provide on-demand deliveries, reducing waste and oversupply • Leveraging technology (such as text messages) can reduce the need for infrastructure • Failing to consider relevant stakeholders and regulations (such as flight paths) in the design process can significantly hinder implementation
Aim	Provision of timely medical services in remote and difficult to access locations
Design outcome	Distribution centres for sending medical aid with drones

Table A.6   Driverless ambulances summary

Case study	Driverless ambulances: redirection of aid (p. 32)
Intent	Design for capacity
Typology	System automation
User	Paramedics and patients
Unmet needs	Efficient and resource-effective treatment of patients in low-risk situations
Context	Emergency services are unable to tend to all emergency calls
Insight	• Emergency responses range from low to high risk scenarios • Ambulances are the solution for medical aid outside of hospitals, yet attention is divided and addressing a low-risk medical complication can preclude administering aid in a high-risk situation elsewhere • Low-risk patients could be transported by driverless ambulance to receive care in hospital
Aim	Improve response times to patients in high-risk situations without neglecting low-risk patients
Design outcome	Driverless ambulances to assist in addressing low-risk medical emergencies, thus reducing burden on emergency services

Table A.7   EpiPen summary

Case study	EpiPen: simple and effective design (p. 81)
Intent	Design for empowerment
Typology	Confidence instillers
User	People who administer epinephrine injections
Unmet needs	The ability to confidently self-inject or inject others when needed
Context	Individuals suffering from very serious allergic reactions need to swiftly receive medical attention
Insight	• Easy-to-remember basic instructions can help users recall information in stressful situations • Sharply contrasting colours can help orientation, even for colour-blind individuals • Reducing chance of user error can improve user confidence
Aim	Provide a way to safely and reliably administer adrenaline injection to self or others
Design outcome	EpiPen portable adrenaline injection device allow for a firm grip due to the elliptical shape. The instructions are printed on the device and separated into three simple, visual steps. The use of colour (blue safety-release cap and orange needle protector) aids in recalling the instructions 'Blue to the sky. Orange in the thigh'

Table A.8 HealthMap summary

Case study	HealthMap: disease surveillance (p. 27)
Intent	Design for capacity
Typology	Information systems
User	Global healthcare institutions and individuals
Unmet needs	Live information resource surrounding infectious diseases
Context	Current information dissemination is relatively slow and communicated through traditional media/government outlets
Insight	• Medial threats cannot be treated at the local/national level but by nature must be dealt with at a global scale • A global platform that presents information on medical outbreaks could provide a rapidly updated unbiased source and platform to inform decisions of individuals and medical institutions
Aim	Change the way people interact with infectious diseases—especially in developing countries—to lessen the strain on hospitals
Design outcome	A system and accompanying applications that track public health threats worldwide and send real-time data to users

Table A.9 Hospitable hospice summary

Case study	Hospitable hospice: redefining end-of-life care (p. 45)
Intent	Design for knowledge
Typology	Blueprints
User	Hospices and hospice designers
Unmet needs	Hospices designed to deliver optimal care and an uplifting experience for residents
Context	Significant stigma associated with discussing end-of-life and what it means to have a 'good death'
Insight	• Hospices are complicated, necessitating a range of emotional and physical experiences for varying stakeholders • Designing open access outcomes can create social value and be of benefit to a range of entities and institutions not directly affiliated with the design itself
Aim	Redesign the experience of death and dying in hospices
Design outcome	A handbook that provides a blueprint to guide the design of hospices with a view towards improving the overall experience for patients, caregivers, family and staff members

Table A.10   Ice Bucket Challenge summary

Case study	Ice Bucket Challenge: power of people (p. 47)
Intent	Design for knowledge
Typology	Awareness
User	Wider community and individuals suffering from Amyotrophic Lateral Sclerosis (ALS)
Unmet needs	General awareness of, and treatment for, ALS
Context	ALS not well understand or a research a research priority
Insight	• Social media has enabled campaigns to grow exponentially and generate exposure on a global scale • A 'challenge' format for social media campaigns can foster community participation and encourage donations to a cause
Aim	Increase awareness of ALS and donations to research entities
Design outcome	Viral campaign—Ice Bucket Challenge—to raise awareness and funds for treating ALS

Table A.11   Incubators summary

Case study	Incubators: one size does not fit all (p. 87)
Intent	Design for empowerment
Typology	Experiential design
User	Mothers and medical staff caring for newborns requiring incubation
Unmet needs	Context-specific incubators that address a host of user needs and misconceptions
Context	Incubators for low-resource hospitals with inexperienced staff or carers
Insight	• Nursing staff would often place multiple babies under incubator UV lights when they were born with jaundice—this left much of the baby's body under-exposed to the light • Concerned nurses would sometimes cover incubators with blankets for warmth but this would block UV light from reaching the jaundiced baby's skin • Centralised incubator positioning in a ward decreased the amount of bonding time between parent and child
Aim	Incubators that are mobile and difficult for nursing staff or parents to misuse
Design outcome	A range of incubators (i.e. Firefly, NeoNurture and BabyBloom) that address needs in different sociocultural contexts

Table A.12 Kitten Scanner summary

Case study	Kitten Scanner: addressing a child's fears and anxiety (p. 85)
Intent	Design for empowerment
Typology	Experiential design
User	Children requiring an MRI scan
Unmet needs	Distracting and relaxing children from the unfamiliar environment and MRI scan procedure
Context	Children face significant anxiety when visiting waiting rooms within the hospital environment and during medical procedures (such as getting an MRI scan)
Insight	• Interactivity, story-telling, and immediate feedback can create a positive experience for children and help combat anxiety during medical procedures
	• Simulating medical producers (such as a scan) with toys can help prepare children and create positive associations with the equipment and caregivers
Aim	Transform the way children interact with MRI systems and reduce anxiety prior to and during the process
Design outcome	An interactive,scaled-down and stylised model of a CT scanner which can assist a child to learn about the MRI procedure, thus reducing anxiety during the procedure

Table A.13 Liftware summary

Case study	Liftware: eating with stability (p. 76)
Intent	Design for empowerment
Typology	Promoting ability
User	People who suffer from hand tremors and/or have limited hand and arm mobility
Unmet needs	Ways for individuals with limited hand-arm mobility or hand tremors to eat independently and with dignity
Context	Individuals which are unable to handle cutlery on their own often rely on carers to aid in eating
Insight	• Sensors and drivers can counteract unwanted shaking motion and limited mobility to keep the head of a utensil steady and level to avoid spillage
	• Provision of interchangeable utensil heads widens the utility of a device
Aim	To promote confidence and independence while eating for people with hand tremors or have limited hand mobility
Design outcome	Liftware—a stabilising and levelling product with attachments that assits people to eat

Table A.14   Nurse handover summary

Case study	Nurse handover: new procedures for increasing accuracy (p. 33)
Intent	Design for capacity
Typology	Efficiency innovations
User	Nurses
Unmet needs	Efficient patient information handovers between shifts
Context	No standardised process for nurses to debrief oncoming shift staff, resulting in long handover periods after shift has ended and information being missed
Insight	• Previous handovers lacked structure and occurred in isolation from the patients • Information was often exchanged verbally without consistent record-keeping • Patients might need to repeat information or correct information • Mobile devices and applications can facilitate structured record-keeping on the move
Aim	To speed up and improve the accuracy of patient-information handovers
Design outcome	Portable software device with specific patient notes to allow for pre-population of key information, and to allow handovers to be inclusive of patients

Table A.15   Packaging pills summary

Case study	Packaging pills: tracking intake (p. 49)
Intent	Design for knowledge
Typology	Visual communication
User	Medication users
Unmet needs	Accessible pill packaging with legible information
Context	Poor design of pill bottles can lead to incorrect dosage of prescription medication or taking the wrong medicine
Insight	• Confidence in dosage tracking can reduce error • Larger labels placed on a flat surface are more easily legible and can help to prioritise key information • Interchangeable coloured bands can help differentiate between similar bottles and prevent people from taking medication belonging to others
Aim	Reduce human error with prescription medication
Design outcome	ClearRx 'D-shaped' pill bottle allowing for a large label and colour bands to help differentiate pill bottles and manage dosage

Table A.16 Pap smear speculum summary

Case study	Pap smear speculum: moving beyond the duck bill (p. 62)
Intent	Design for enablement
Typology	Procedural instruments
User	Pap smear patients
Unmet needs	Comfortable experience prior to and during pap smears
Context	Speculums originally designed as one size fits all with a focus on the clinician rather than the patient
Insight	• Pap smear procedures often leave patients uncomfortable, tense and embarrassed
	• A lack of introduction, explanation, and warning can contribute to a negative pap smear experience
	• Appropriate material selection can reduce issues and, improve patient comfort without compromising a doctor's ability; silicone covered metal used to reduce mechanical noise and replace the cold feeling of being touched by a metal instrument
	• Mobile applications with information, reminders, encouragement, and clarity on results can improve the patient experience
Aim	Make the pap smear experience more relaxing, empathetic, and even light-hearted
Design outcome	Redesigned speculum and interaction to improve patient comfort and reduce anxiety

Table A.17 Rescue Rashie summary

Case study	Rescue Rashie: instructions where they are needed (p. 51)
Intent	Design for knowledge
Typology	Visual communication
User	Individuals providing CPR to children
Unmet needs	Accessible, general knowledge on providing CPR
Context	It can be difficult to recall information in high-stress situation where a life is at stake
Insight	• Providing simple and easy-to-understand guide in the context of use can help inform and prepare an untrained individual
	• Instructions should be easily accessible and easy to interpret
Aim	Provision of guidance for performing CPR on a child when necessary
Design outcome	Rescue rashie, a shirt that is worn when a child is swimming, featuring CPR instructions behind a zipped flap on the front of the garment

Table A.18 U Scope summary

Case study	U Scope: modernising a symbol of healthcare (p. 66)
Intent	Design for enablement
Typology	Diagnostics
User	Medical practitioners
Unmet needs	Ergonomic and usability upgrades to standard stethoscopes
Context	The basic concept of the stethoscope has not changed since the nineteenth century. Prolonged use of current design can result in ear-aches and neck pain
Insight	• An age-old design isn't synonymous with perfection, it is important to challenge assumptions and norms • Redesign of key features (such as modified earpiece joints and a balanced grip) can significantly enhance usability • Providing alternative ways for wear can better suit different users (e.g. reducing the size to enable pocket-carrying rather than neck-hanging) • Options for personalisation can elicit positive experiences for the user by creating a luxury feel
Aim	Re-design the stethoscope to improve doctor's comfort and ability to use the product for a prolonged period
Design outcome	A stethoscope reduces ear pressure, is pocket-sized and can be personalised

Table A.19 SnowWorld summary

Case study	SnowWorld: distraction with virtual reality (p. 86)
Intent	Design for empowerment
Typology	Experiential design
User	Burn victims
Unmet needs	Effective pain management during treatment of burn wounds
Context	Patients with burn wounds are under significant pain during wound care and painkillers are sometimes insufficient for mitigating this pain
Insight	• Virtual reality can create immersive experiences which divert the users attention from their immediate surroundings • Immersing burn patients in a virtual world of cold, snowy conditions can distract them significantly from the pain of severe burns
Aim	To distract patients from pain through an experience that is the polar opposite
Design outcome	SnowWorld virtual reality game that distracts patients from pain during burn treatment and recovery

Table A.20 Tango Belt Summary

Case study	Tango Belt: reducing the fear and impact of falls (p. 82)
Intent	Design for empowerment
Typology	Confidence instillers
User	Elderly people susceptible to falls
Unmet needs	Increased mobility and confidence for elderly individuals susceptible to falls
Context	Elderly people can be at high risk of falling, and a resulting hip fracture can be difficult to recover from
Insight	• Ergonomic and primary observational data showed reduced confidence and mobility when at risk • Elderly individuals had poor compliance with the device due to associated stigma • Patients with improved confidence lead to an increase in mobility
Aim	Reduce the impact of falls
Design outcome	A smart belt that employs motion-sensing technology to detect a fall that is likely to result in a hip impact. When such a fall is sensed, the belt activates an air-bag to lessen the impact of a fall on the hip

Table A.21 Thrive Project summary

Case study	Thrive Project: perceptions of hospitals (p. 44)
Intent	Design for knowledge
Typology	Blueprints
User	Patients in children's hospital
Unmet needs	Calming ward environment that meets the experiential and emotional needs of stakeholders
Context	Children and their families can feel intimidated and isolated during hospital stays
Insight	• A calm and supportive environment for patients is a critical component of health care services • By promoting togetherness, perceptions of the hospital environment can be changed, particularly for children • Co-design with patients and families can lead to better solutions for meeting their explicit and latent needs • The use of ambient lights and sound technologies can reduce patient anxiety
Aim	Provide a happier and healthier hospital experience for patients and staff
Design outcome	An interactive and fun hospital environment for staff, patients, and families

Table A.22 TickleFLEX summary

Case study	TickleFLEX: insulin injection aid (p. 79)
Intent	Design for empowerment
Typology	Promoting ability
User	Diabetic patients
Unmet needs	An easy self-injection experience which prevents insulin leakage
Context	Some patients dread their daily insulin injections
Insight	• Previous developments have focused on the needle, rather than the full experience of injection • Key issues with daily self-injection include avoiding nerves and muscles, and achieving a steady injection without repeated attempts • When a patient is confident about one injection site, they might re-use it until scar tissue makes it too difficult and painful to be used further • Concealing the needle during injection can help people with needle phobia cope
Aim	Make self-injection more consistent, comfortable and less stressful
Design outcome	Low-cost, single-component TickleFLEX is a self-injection aid which gently gathers and secures the skin to proivde a steady hold for the needle to enter. The aid also conceals the needle during the entire injection process

Table A.23 Tovertafel dementia games summary

Case study	Tovertafel dementia games: a sense of connection (p. 84)
Intent	Design for empowerment
Typology	Experiential design
User	Dementia sufferers and their families
Unmet needs	Sense of connection for individuals with dementia in residential care
Context	Many dementia sufferers feel isolated and lonely in residential care
Insight	• There is no cure for dementia, so current treatments for dementia take the form of symptom management • Engagements should avoid alienating the patients from their familiar surroundings • Solutions for individuals with dementia should stimulate physical and cognitive functions for maximum effectiveness
Aim	Comfort and stimulus for patients through social engagement in their care environment
Design outcome	Tovertafel Original, enables a connection among elderly people in the late stages of dementia by projecting a variety of games onto a table or flat surface. Sensors, speakers and processors work together to create a stimulating physical and cognitive environment

Table A.24   Trocar summary

Case study	Trocar: not just about function (p. 59)
Intent	Design for enablement
Typology	Procedural instruments
User	Surgeons and hospitals
Unmet needs	Affordable and sustainable trocar design
Context	Trocars are disposable and often single-use, which has led to high costs and waste
Insight	• 'Resposable' products offer a way of making the core product re-usable, with only components necessitating disposal being discarded • Universal seals could allow for interchangeable instruments and reduce costs
Aim	Reduce costs and waste associated with trocars
Design outcome	YelloPort Elite, a largely resuable trocar with only one key component requiring replacement. The universal port also allows a range of different trocar tips and sizes to be used and changed easily

Table A.25   Ultrasound machines summary

Case study	Ultrasound machines: where and when you need a diagnosis (p. 67)
Intent	Design for enablement
Typology	Diagnostics
User	Doctors preforming an ultrasound outside of a hospital
Unmet needs	Portable ultrasound systems for use in remote or rural contexts, or in situations with difficult access
Context	Despite a range of technical advancements, ultrasound machines required a hospital environment, limiting portability and the context of use
Insight	• Mobile ultrasound machines could allow scans to be performed in new situations like ambulances, in rural locations, during bedside assessments and in smaller general practices
Aim	Access to ultrasound scanning outside of a hospital environment
Design outcome	Lumify, consisting of a portable handheld tele-ultrasound device, mobile application and plug-in transducer to share images and videos from an ultrasound in real time

Table A.26   World's Greatest Shave summary

Case study	World's Greatest Shave: inclusion through empathy (p. 48)
Intent	Design for knowledge
Typology	Awareness
User	Wider community and individuals with blood cancer
Unmet needs	Blood cancer awareness
Context	Leukaemia is cancer of the blood which is often fatal
Insight	• Social media is an excellent channel for promoting campaigns to large audiences • Through personalised marketing, people all over the world feel involved with the campaign through combinations of donation and participation
Aim	Increase donations and awareness of blood cancers and the Leukaemia Foundation
Design outcome	The World's Greatest Shave, a global campaign that encourages people to either shave or dye their hair to promote awareness and donations for leukemia research

Table A.27   Wong-Baker FACES Pain Rating Scale summary

Case study	Wong-Baker FACES Pain Rating Scale: giving pain a face (p. 65)
Intent	Design for enablement
Typology	Diagnostics
User	Medical practitioners and patients
Unmet needs	Patients can find it difficult to verbally convey how much pain they are in
Context	Existing methods to determine the degree of pain experienced by a patient were not particularly effective for children or when language barriers were present
Insight	• Values used to communicate degree of pain were not universal, effective, or efficient for child patients • Use of graphics (i.e. emotive and graphical facial expressions) provided a more effective method of communicating between doctors and several patient groups
Aim	Create a more efficient and accurate process for pain communication between patients and medical staff
Design outcome	Wong-Baker Pain Scale consisting of six different pain levels represented by visual facial expressions